The PEOPLE DIMENSION

Managing the Transition to World-Class Manufacturing

The PEOPLE DIMENSION

Managing the Transition to World-Class Manufacturing

Ronald J. Recardo   Luigi A. Peluso

QUALITY RESOURCES
A Division of The Kraus Organization Limited
White Plains, New York

Printed in the United States of America

96 95 94 93 92   10 9 8 7 6 5 4 3 2 1

Quality Resources
A Division of The Kraus Organization Limited
One Water Street
White Plains, New York 10601

The paper used in this publication meets the minimum requirements of American National Standard for Information Sciences—Permanence of Paper for Printed Library Materials, ANSI Z39.48-1984.

ISBN 0-527-91666-8

Library of Congress Cataloging-in-Publication Data

Recardo, Ronald J.
    The people dimension : managing the transition to world-class manufacturing / Ronald J. Recardo, Luigi A. Peluso.
        p. cm.
    Includes index.
    ISBN 0-527-91666-8 (acid-free)
    1. United States—Manufactures—Management. I. Peluso, Luigi A.
II. Title.
HD9725.R43 1992
670'.68—dc20   92-11950
                                                       CIP

Contents

Acknowledgments

This book is written for managers, internal change agents, and internal consultants who are either contemplating a change initiative or who are currently involved in a transition that has yielded less than the expected results. I hope this book will provide some new insights and will identify an approach that can be used by a manufacturing company to achieve world-class performance.

Numerous individuals have played direct and indirect roles in the writing of this book. My early knowledge of change management is to a large extent due to the projects I worked on while employed at Arthur Andersen & Company. I am indebted to several partners and managers for providing me with an opportunity to take a lead role in the development of their firmwide Organization Change Methodology. This provided me with extensive conceptual and "hands on" experience in planning and implementing large-scale organizational changes.

I would also like to thank Kenneth McGuire, the founder of Manufacturing Excellence Action Coalition. As my mentor at MEAC he gave me the opportunity to incorporate my ideas into MEAC's World Class Manufacturing practice. His counsel on the application of Japanese manufacturing principles to manufacturing companies in the U.S. was instrumental in the development of my operational expertise. I will forever be indebted to him for giving me the opportunity to work with the outstanding personnel of MEAC and its distinguished client base.

Although I have been associated with Wm. A. Schiemann & Associates, Inc., for only a short time, I would like to thank Bill Schiemann, James Shillaber, and John Lingle for being sounding boards and for helping me to develop further the concepts in this book. No doubt, as we continue to apply these concepts to a broader client base, our approach will be further defined.

And last, but certainly not least, I would like to thank my family. The love, support, and sacrifice of my parents, John and Mary Recardo, instilled in me a strong work ethic and the desire to set and achieve high goals. I would like to dedicate this book to my best friend and wife, Sandy. She has, for the past seven years, shared in my dreams, my achievements, and my disappointments. Through the years Sandy has *always* been my number one supporter and has believed in me, at times, more than I believed in my own capabilities. Without her, any success I ever achieve would be meaningless.

Ronald J. Recardo

*   *   *   *   *

To my wife, Lisa, for her selfless support and patience.

My special thanks to Kenneth J. McGuire, president and founder of Manufacturing Excellence Action Coalition, for his generosity in sharing a life's worth of insight and knowledge. It is a gift which will be impossible to repay.

Luigi A. Peluso

Introduction

How many times have you heard the following statement?

People are our most valuable asset.

Few individuals in any organization would question its validity. But, take a moment really to think about the significance of this seemingly simple and yet surprisingly obscure proposition.

Regardless of what the technological theorists have been envisioning for several years, we have not quite figured out how to run our various businesses without people. Much to our dismay, many of the high-tech gadgets we have developed and invested in very heavily are not bringing quite the returns we had hoped for. The idea behind much of the gadgetry was to simplify the task of management by reducing human involvement via mechanization. The marketers of these instruments have been quite successful in convincing us of the benefits of reducing or, better yet, eliminating human judgment within our operations.

It is true that automation and the computer have completely changed the face of the business world. Over time, those organizations that do not learn how to manage and intelligently apply technology will be victims of it. The distinguishing factor between winners and losers will be the ability to identify and to utilize those tools that will assist the organization's people in delivering results that exceed customer expectations. We emphasize that the winner's approach will be to maximize its employees' effectiveness, not to minimize the number of employees. So, for the foreseeable future, we are going to have to learn how to deal with the folks we have working in our various facilities.

Managing Human Assets

The irony in our opening statement is that although everyone is willing to accept it at face value, very few companies have demonstrated proficiency in human asset management!

For some organizations, the concept of people as an asset may take some getting used to and may, in fact, require some imagination. If you don't believe this, we would suggest that you suspend your skepticism until after you have subjected your company to an objective assessment.

To start with, not all of these "assets" are equal in value or simple to assess. For some mysterious reason the recruitment guidelines many organizations apply to their salaried workforce do not apply to the direct and indirect workers: minor things like the ability to speak English, to read at a sixth-grade level, or to perform four-function math. Even the classification of the workforce supports a subliminal value system, or class system. Let's take a look at some typical designations to clarify this point.

Is your workforce made up of "white-collar" and "blue-collar" workers? How is this terminology reflected in the company communications? How does this impact people's sense of worth? A second common segregation is value-adding and non-value-adding employees. What management system actually adheres to the belief that some employees don't add value to the company or the products? If this is really the case, then why are these people on the payroll? What if you were a "non-value-adding" employee? Wouldn't you be delighted to explain to your family exactly what a "non-value-adding" employee of the company does? The same type of twisted-logic classification holds true for direct versus indirect laborers. We have wondered on a couple of occasions exactly what "exempt" employees are exempt from (other than the pleasures of punching a time clock). Kenneth J. McGuire, President of the Manufacturing Excellence Action Coalition, once put it this way: "We call people 'hourly' workers as if we made a decision, on whether or not we are going to keep them, on an hour by hour basis." So much for fostering loyalty and a sense of pride.

This "class system" is in absolute contradiction to the team environment many American companies are trying so desperately to foster. The financial disparity between the levels of the organization is a national embarassment. For example, top U.S. automobile company executives have been criticized by the Japanese, and by many Americans, for the very large salaries they are paid despite the dismal performance of their companies.

In a manufacturing company, is any function genuinely more important than any other? Manufacturing, as a business, is a complex chain of events in which materials are transformed into a higher state of value and placed in a distribution system that converts them into revenue. This process is evident regardless of the complexity of the product or the size of the organization. The chain of events requires a support mechanism of some type. No link is unimportant; every link must be strong. Take a good look at your organization. How do you know for sure where the weak links are?

Many manufacturers believe that they are weak in the operational workforce. If the hiring practices for these hourly jobs have been unselective, such concerns are valid. For far too long American factories have been employing people in the shop whom they would never consider for any other position within the company. Now, suddenly we want to "empower" these people to catapult the company to world-class performance.

The tragedy is that American management has developed a mentality that views these people as bodies with virtual disregard for their minds, and has developed the systems to control them accordingly. Our mass-production mentality, coupled with mass-market demands, fueled this management philosophy. We designed factories where people did not have to communicate with one another. This made the cultural and language differences tolerable. Factories and businesses learned how to move ahead. Whether the shop folks contributed or not seemed irrelevant. America climbed to the top of the industrial world—for a while.

Part of this great feat was the tuning of our operations to the point where not much intelligence was needed in the factory. We looked to idiot-proof jobs so that, for all practical purposes, idiots could do them. We conditioned people to become specialists to maximize their individual efficiency at the cost of flexibility (for which we might have had to pay them more money).

Adapting to the Times

The fact is that business demands have changed from mass production serving mass markets to high flexibility for serving multiple narrow market segments. We find ourselves unable to run in today's race with the machine we created over the last century or so. Now what?

The United States no longer sits comfortably on top of the hill. American manufacturers have taken our leadership position and our competitors for granted. Like spoiled children, we have grown and squandered our inheritance. We have come to the realization that we have managed our way off the pinnacle. We milked the assets we acquired to squeeze out a few more pennies per share in profits. We neglected to improve ourselves continuously. Along the way we forgot to reinvest in many of our most valuable assets, especially people. The further down the ladder and the further out of sight those assets were, the less time and money we spent on them.

American management is awakening to realize that, unlike hard assets that depreciate in value, employees can appreciate in worth to their organizations. The office and the factory floor of every manufacturing company offer an enormous potential opportunity. This opportunity rests on the ability to harness the minds, as well as the bodies, of the masses. No machine has the flexibility or the capability of a human being.

A Balanced Approach

Management's charge is to execute a strategy that will transform its workforce into a competitive weapon. This will require very different skills and mindsets at every level of the organization. We must rethink all aspects of running a manufacturing company. The driving force behind a change of this magnitude is, quite simply, survival.

The United States is a trendy and often fad-crazed nation. Manufacturing management, like the population in general, loves to ride the current wave. It seems as though every pet rock, hula hoop, or CB radio has had a counterpart in manufacturing. The seeds for these fads seem to be planted by articles in our beloved business journals. The momentum builds as scattered reports of dizzying achievements get increased visibility. Suddenly it seems impossible to pick up a magazine that does not have an article or editorial on whatever the current topic may be. Fear of possibly missing out leads to frantic and haphazard attempts at implementation. Most of these programs die on the vine at the hands of amateurs. A majority of them cause disillusionment with what might be a valid concept. Each attempt serves only to undermine the chances of success for the next new program.

We have clients who refer to this management phenomenon as "MBMA"—which stands for Management By Magazine Article. The results are typically what you would expect of any initiative where the misinformed lead the uninformed on a misdirected crusade. We have also heard this management style called the "idea of the month."

To find possible explanations for this phenomenon, we need not look further than our national pastime. Baseball is an American institution. We love to watch our heroes smash home runs. It's far more exciting to watch a team snatch victory from the jaws of defeat by one big smack than it is to watch a team win by scoring runs off a lot of singles. We have immortalized the words of Yogi Berra, "It ain't over till it's over."

American companies seem intent on managing their businesses the same way. Rather than sweat out many small successes, with all the players, we wait for that meatball pitch the hero can belt out of the park for the game-winning run. We do so despite the fact that it's a long shot. Somehow we think that success is sweeter if we have overcome adversity to get it.

In the game of manufacturing, the rules keep changing. We hope to provide you with the strategies and tactics you are going to need to remain in contention. They represent what the best teams in the game are using to get (and stay) ahead. This book is not about how to hit home runs, it's about how to play nine innings and get the most out of your players.

The Plan of the Book

Just as no championship team can afford to rely on a single play, a world-class manufacturer will need to be strong all around. We are strong advocates of a balanced approach to meaningful and lasting change. This book will help identify the philosophical, technical, and people aspects that need to come together to win in the 1990s. It will help you understand how the pieces fit together and how to manage the transition to world-class performance. The synchromization of these elements is mandatory for success.

The first three chapters discuss competition, strategies for survival, and productivity. We assess the effect of global competitiveness on our standard of living and why recent trends show cause for concern. We explain the impact of new technology and market segmentation on most manufacturing companies. Our intent is to frame the strategies that a manufacturing company must adopt to become competitive in today's global economic storm.

We have found that genuinely world-class companies are focusing on the tactical principles that support fundamental strategies. Their focus is on Total Quality Management, Just In Time Manufacturing, and administrative productivity improvement. Each initiative impacts, and is dependent on, the other two. Taken together, they refine the efficiency, productivity, and performance of the entire company.

Chapters 4 through 6 spell out the key success factors for achieving and sustaining supremacy in the global marketplace. These human factors deal with employee involvement and the integration of all company functions and systems. They shed light on the areas that trip up most companies that charge blindly ahead. They provide insight on the areas of reward and recognition as well as communication and education that many companies overlook. Without these elements to cement progress, even the most well-thought-out plans and realized benefits will gradually dwindle away. The absence of these critical aspects is the reason why many past efforts seem to just disappear.

The seventh chapter provides the foundational methodology to execute and successfully manage the transition as you move along. We have presented a map by which an individual company can chart a journey. The charted course along the map must be unique to each company because no two companies start from the same point. No two have the same capabilities. Unfortunately, there are no cookbook solutions.

We would like to emphasize that although the individual concepts we talk about seem simple, their correct application is not. Manufacturing is flooded with "also-ran" companies. Be advised that as you move forward through the pack, the number of failures around you will be dwarfed by the number of fakers with a good story. Time will differentiate those who really did from those who merely say they did.

Global Market Warfare

Every day the world becomes a smaller place. We are living in a time of unprecedented political, social, and economic change. World events and changes put more and more pressure on the global economic infrastructure. This force is manifesting itself in the form of genuinely global competition.

How Does the United States Stack Up?

Manufacturers in the United States are being pressed to perform and compete in the world economy. Among our major competitors are the United Kingdom, Japan, Germany, Canada, France, and Italy. Together with the United States, these nations comprise the Summit Seven. It is interesting to note how the United States compares to its Summit Seven partners. According to the Council on Competitiveness, there are four general economic indicators that can be used: investment, manufacturing productivity, trade, and standard of living. These indices can help gauge, in relative terms, where the United States stands.

1

Investment

The foundation of competitiveness is investment. This basic measure plays an important role in future preparedness. Investment impacts the three other competitive measures significantly. It represents our nation's expenditures on plant, equipment, education, and research and development. Figure 1.1 shows a weighted average of national expenditures on plant and equipment.

In 1989, Japan spent 23.6 percent of its gross domestic product on plant and equipment. It was the first time since World War II that any country had invested more, in absolute terms, than the United States in plant and equipment. The gap was $36 billion. The United States invested $513 billion against Japan's $549 billion. This is in spite of the fact that the American GDP in 1989 was more than double that of Japan. At these levels of spending, is it really any wonder that Japan's manufacturing base has become one of the most modern, efficient, and competitive in the world? For the last twenty years, U.S. private in-

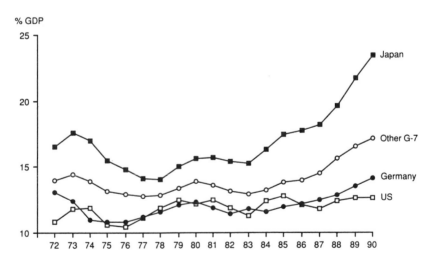

FIGURE 1.1. Private industry expenditures on plant and equipment.

SOURCE: Council on Competitiveness and OECD National Accounts.

vestment, as a percentage of gross domestic product, in plant and equipment, has fallen below the average for the other Summit Seven. With investment as a foundational element of future competitiveness, this trend is quite disturbing.

Figure 1.2 reflects long-term trends in educational investment. The United States has arguably the finest university system in the world. This point is quite clearly reflected in the large number of foreign students and faculty who come into our system. Over 50 percent of the students currently enrolled in Ph.D. programs in the hard sciences are foreign nationals. America has one of the highest GDP spending levels in the world on education. Unfortunately, although we do not have an investment shortfall, we do have a performance shortfall. American students do not seem to perform well on internationally standardized math and science tests. There is considerable debate over why this is so, and it is a topic that is beyond the scope of this book. Our high dropout rate should be of concern to us all. Industry has attempted to bring some attention to the problem of inadequately prepared graduates. And shortages of workers with sufficient math and

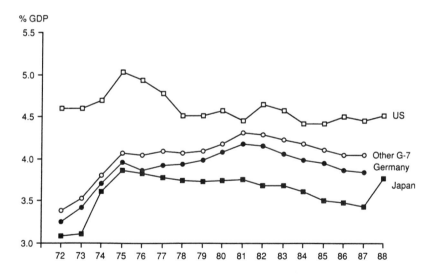

FIGURE 1.2.   Government expenditure on education.

Source: Council on Competitiveness and OECD National Accounts.

science skills present a severe constraint on our future ability to compete.

One of the advantages the United States does have is that our educational system is flexible in structure relative to those of many industrialized nations. However, even if our school system underwent a revolutionary beneficial change today, it would take 13 to 16 years for its products to become available to industry. None of us can afford to wait. The private sector has no choice but to educate its existing workforce. This education will, at a minimum, need to give the people the skills to meet today's competitive environment. Those organizations that do not rise to meet this educational obligation, and that must compete in a global arena, will simply cease to exist.

Productivity

Manufacturing productivity is affected by many factors. Among these factors are the type and condition of the equipment being used. Another factor has to do with how well the people are performing. In the United States, manufacturing represents about one-fifth of the total gross domestic product. Manufacturing also represents a significant portion of this country's trade. Figure 1.3 shows the trend in productivity from 1972 to 1989.

From 1974 to 1982 the United States averaged a 1 percent annual growth in productivity. During the same period, West Germany clicked along at over twice that rate. Figure 1.3 demonstrates that Japan experienced an annual productivity increase of 5.3 percent.

The good news is that from 1983 to 1987 the United States was able to boost its productivity rate by 5.7 percent. This has been a significant step in the right direction. Concern in the United States has been high and more companies are striving to get their productivity up. The bad news is that the Japanese were able to shoot up in 1987 alone by a rate of 8.4 percent. It does not take a Ph.D. in economics to see that the difference in rates of productivity improvement spells trouble for the United States.

Trade

With the world seemingly becoming smaller, the ability to trade in world markets is fundamental to both company and national income.

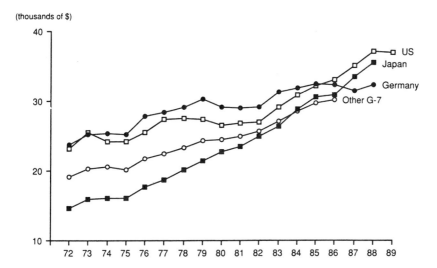

FIGURE 1.3. GDP per manufacturing employee (constant 1980 dollars).

Source: Council on Competitiveness and OECD National Accounts.

In many instances trade performance can be linked to final product cost. Since product cost is typically a function of productivity, the connection can be made between manufacturing productivity and trade. The United States' success in world markets can be measured by its share of worldwide exports. Figure 1.4 depicts the long-term trends in trade from 1972 to 1990.

The graph shows the United States as one of the main exporters of manufactured goods. Our 1990 sales exports were in excess of $280 billion. The U.S. resurgence since 1985 has been aided by the international devaluation of the dollar. Our agricultural products, along with technology products in the aerospace, pharmaceutical, chemical, and scientific equipment, fueled our drive to the top. But even with our record exports, we have had a $100 billion trade deficit each year since 1984. As a nation we continue to rely on imported goods.

The swings in international currency have made imported products relatively more expensive in the United States. This quite clearly shows

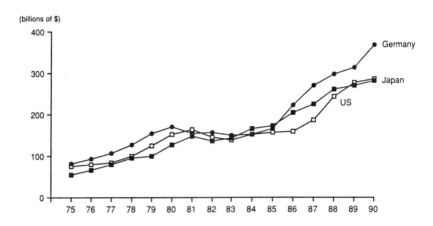

FIGURE 1.4.   Manufactured goods exports (current dollars).

Source: Council on Competitiveness and OECD National Accounts.

that the American consumer perceives those imported goods to have more value than the less expensive domestic products. This points to competitive deficiencies that go beyond price tag alone. In the international market, quality and value warrant premium price.

Standard of Living

The fourth index is the standard of living. Our standard of living is how we gauge how we're doing in our pocketbooks. The individual's income, as well as the nation's, will determine the number of financial choices we have relative to our foreign counterparts. Figure 1.5 shows the standard of living in terms of GDP per person from 1972 thru 1990.

The graph shows Germany at the top, where it has been for quite a while. The United States is in second place, over the average of the remaining Summit Seven. Our rate of income has been steadily creeping up since 1972. But in comparison to the rate of change of our competitors we have been moving slowly. The rate of change has been only a fraction of what the Germans and Japanese have enjoyed. Our influence and buying power are soon going to be less of a factor in the world's economy than they were in the past.

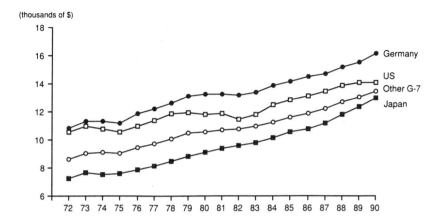

FIGURE 1.5.   GDP per capita (constant 1980 dollars).

SOURCE: Council on Competitiveness and OECD National Accounts.

Figures 1.1 through 1.5 display what has been going on in quantitative form. Let us take a look now in a slightly less scientific manner. The first place to look is in the driveway or parking lot. What has been happening relative to trade is quite clear from the number of foreign cars there. When we go into the typical American living room, the point is even more obvious. Here we find televisions, stereos, and assorted other electronic goodies whose manufacture has long since gone offshore.

Japan, Inc.

In the sixth century B.C. Sun Tzu wrote: "If you know the enemy and know yourself, you need not fear the result of a hundred battles." Many U.S. manufacturers would have been wise to heed Sun Tzu's advice. The leader and most formidable competitor in manufacturing is Japan. Despite its devastating industrial capability, Japan is a country about which we continue to know very little. As a nation, we have appeared to be content with a modest level of understanding. Much of our knowledge unfortunately is based on myths and theory rather than on fact. Our continued inability to deal with Japan politically is creating stress on the entire world's system of balance.

Japan has about one-half the population of the United States. Its land area is approximately the same as that of California. Because of its mountainous geography, much of the land in Japan is economically infeasible to develop. It has no raw materials to speak of and limited energy resources. Both of these supply-side issues make the cost of operating a manufacturing business staggering. The most affordable and readily available resource, until fairly recently, has been labor. Japan's domestic market is insufficient to support its own output. Therefore, exporting products is a necessity for survival.

Japan is strong in several critical aspects. First, it has access to very patient, low-cost capital. Many of Japan's largest manufacturers are closely tied to banks through bidirectional equity positions. This allows companies to take quite a different perspective on new business opportunities than an American counterpart may be able to afford. They look at long-term growth. We want short-term results. As long as we continue to allow Wall Street to determine how companies are run, we will be forced to cry about unfair foreign competition. "Fair" is however the competitor who is winning decides to leverage his strength.

Second, the Japanese have become masters at creating highly efficient manufacturing systems. This skill can be attributed to their restrictive physical environmental and economic constraints. The Japanese seek to maintain low overhead costs by leveraging each employee's contribution. The labor pool is quite stable and continues to increase in overall skill sets. We are all products of our environment and, as such, the Japanese are products of a fiercely competitive domestic market.

The Japanese are not perfect, however: their knowledge of international distribution systems is far below their production knowhow. The Japanese have to contend with a high fixed cost of operations whose organizational structure is quite rigid. They must deal with high, variable labor costs, and, because of the geography, infrastructure, and population, they must manage a very difficult logistic situation to get supplies.

There are several theories on why Japan is so successful. One theory holds that the Japanese are a benevolent, homogeneous society. The group moves forward on the basis of consensus with a shared national purpose of growth. A second popular theory is that Japan is deliberately enforcing industrial priorities. Part of this theory is the creation of a network of suppliers united within a corporate family to assist one another. It also depicts the Japanese government and foreign ministry as assistants to industry in targeting specific markets for dominance. Unfortunately, both popular theories are fairly accurate.

We believe that there are fundamentally four principles that have allowed Japan to progress from the stature of a defeated nation to become the standard of performance by which all manufacturers will be measured. The adoption of these principles is critical to the success of any manufacturing company in the world. The four principles themselves are simple. Their implications, if executed well, can dramatically improve productivity and therefore competitiveness.

The first principle is that waste is evil. In Japan one of the most precious commodities is space. The Japanese were forced to develop methods of production with little or no waste. At the most elementary level, there simply would not be enough room to store excesses of any kind. The Japanese have found that inventory is the shadow of inefficiency in manufacturing. They look at inventory levels to gauge progress. Their drive to survive hinges on their efficiency. This is why they so vehemently push to get inventory out of their systems.

Principle number two is that a defect is a treasure. It is seen as an opportunity to solve the root cause of a problem. Once fixed, that defect will never occur again. Each problem solved brings them one step closer to perfection. Contrast this to the events that occur when a defect is found in a Western factory where a problem is usually either denied, brushed over with excuses, or temporarily fixed.

The third principle is the continued pursuit of excellence. This involves the never-ending and obsessive search for improvements within the entire organization. The Japanese genuinely believe perfection is possible and drive toward that goal.

Fourth is the principle of worker participation: the first three principles rely on the workers to make them happen. The organization cannot achieve its ultimate goal unless each of its employees is moving ahead. The company depends on its workers and seeks to develop each one as the foundation of a competitive strategy.

Micro Marketing

We are in an era of market segmentation. The days when companies could afford, like Henry Ford, to offer the public "any color, as long as it's black," are gone forever. Companies have striven to differentiate themselves from one another and have sought to reduce competition by focusing on market niches. The first example we can think of is the creation of thousands of different types of athletic footwear (once simply called "sneakers") to meet the needs of a seemingly endless array of activities. Another example is Seiko, which considers itself in the fashion business and, as such, can introduce three new watches a day!

It seems that no market has been able to avoid this trend. Perhaps one of the most intriguing, and well-publicized, examples was Frank Perdue's segmentation of the poultry market. If it can be done with chickens, then no industrial market is safe from marketing's splintering sword. Consumers and customers today are more demanding than ever. As the benefactors of market segmentation, we would no sooner accept telephones that were all black than we would chickens with small breasts. For far too long consumers had little choice as to what they were able to get. Very few suppliers were asking the right questions and even fewer were really listening to the answers.

Then along came the 1980s when getting "market-oriented" became fashionable. And with the solicitation of customers to offer requests, the race was on. The supplier/customer relationship changed profoundly. Not only were customers' demands being both heard and met, but a lot of companies were now asking.

The market was forever changed from plain vanilla to specials. In addition to the changes in the products themselves, customers also had the pick of a whole new breed of suppliers. These suppliers emerged from around the world and were able to compete on cost, quality, and delivery, as well as on responsiveness. The shock to American manufacturers was that the new competitors could compete on these variables simultaneously.

The ability to do so was counter to almost every principle U.S. manufacturing management had held as truth. Among these traditional principles was that product quality was proportionate to product cost. Another was that the only way to shorten lead time was to hold inventory. It was commonly accepted that, to be efficient, plants had to maximize equipment utilization and reduce asset idleness.

Even today there are a large number of American managers who refuse to believe that these trade-offs simply are not true. But with markets accustomed to getting the products they want, at prices and quality levels that they expect, companies will continue to find ways to meet those demands.

Mips, Dips, and Chips

One driver of the segmentation game is technology. We estimate that more technology has been developed in the last fifty years than was developed in the preceding five hundred. The impact of this technological revolution has been the virtually constant increase in complexity of the products we manufacture and purchase.

The dramatic rate of technological advancement impacts both the products and the processes by which they are produced. Advances in communication and transportation have made the world much more accessible. One benefit of this global information availability is heightened awareness of developments in the fields of design and manufacturing. Physical proximity or language barriers can no longer be used as excuses for not knowing what is going on in the world.

It is obvious that the gauge by which all activities will need to be measured is time. Customers and markets are changing almost as fast as they develop. The manufacturers who will be supplying these market segments must be capable of reacting within these dramatically abbreviated time frames.

The inability to react to the changes will expose a front to which more agile competitors will assault. The clear trend that we are witnessing, as a result of this race, is the shortening of product life cycles. It is a trend that has impacted virtually every industrial sector.

Technological innovation is pressing many companies into a literally time-based competition. It shows up in additional features and functions in the products that are being introduced. Companies whose strategy is to compete on a toe-to-toe, punch-to-punch basis are attempting to find new ways to cope in this bell-and-whistle war. Let us take a look at an example that should be familiar: the VCR.

The chances are quite good that the unit in your living room has several features, one of which is quite likely advance programming. The chances are also quite good that you rarely, if ever, use this function. Yet when any of us wander into a store to buy this type of product we tend to want the latest and greatest. This is especially true if the "Turbo" model is priced within our intended range.

The success of the VCR manufacturer, in this case, depends on the ability to provide competitive features at a competitive price. Now imagine that, in six to twelve months, many of the features will need to change to keep pace with the competition. This is a very frightening contest since most manufacturing companies are not skilled in coping with change at an accelerated rate.

In the case of the VCR, the ability to lead or make the technological changes first puts pressure on the rest of the competitive field to react. Simply knowing what modifications to features or functions will be next is insufficient. Success or failure is determined by how well and how quickly the manufacturing process can deal with the changes. The changes may fall into different categories and may impact the technology, output volume, or model mix produced. Flexibility will be among the most valuable traits of any future business enterprise.

Manufacturers are going to have to learn to deal with the market segmentation caused by external changes in demand patterns or technological innovation. These trends will inevitably cause shorter product life cycles. The abbreviation of life cycles will require entirely new organizations and structures with the knowledge and resources to compete against the clock in dynamic world markets.

In addition to advances in product complexity, throughout the world there have been significant changes in production processes themselves. From the standpoint of most U.S. manufacturers, the pursuit of technological advances in production has gone somewhat astray. We have been less successful in attaining measurable results, relative to our foreign competitors, despite the fact that we have more advanced technology.

Automatic Inefficiency

We believe the primary reason why U.S. manufacturers have fallen short is that they have attempted to automate the wrong systems.

Applying automation or advanced technology to an existing, inefficient process or system does not make the overall company any better. The technology has not been integrated with the people systems. The unrestrained application of technological wizardry will actually only consume resources.

We need to simplify our processes and eliminate waste from them, and *then* leverage our technological capability. Compare this to what our most prominent domestic and foreign competitors are doing. In the most successful cases, the winners seem to have simplified their processes and employ technological tools to assist their most flexible resource, people. This is quite different from the normal U.S. mindset, which has been to replace rather than assist people in the manufacturing process. Our traditionally myopic view has resulted in fragments and islands of successful technological and automated experiments. Few companies have genuinely improved their total, end-to-end business cycle and performance by taking this route.

Manufacturers are going to continue to feel the heat of increased competition. The global field of competitors will grow. Just as technology continues to change, so does the political and social climate of many nations. It is the desire of many of these countries to increase their industrial base. They have witnessed the results of Japan's phenomenal growth and success in the world marketplace. They very definitely understand the impact that manufacturing can have on the revitalization of an economy. Nations already on the move include Korea, China, Singapore, and several Eastern and Western European countries.

There is little doubt that the newly industrializing nations will pose a threat as they move forward. We must also keep in mind, however, that our old foes are not just going to go away. The losers will get weeded out, leaving only the best to slug it out.

The changes in markets due to segmentation and technological advances will have people fighting for bigger pieces of smaller pies. Larger companies will not be able to serve their own existence if they do not adopt a truly global outlook. Many of our current foreign competitors are in a better position to capitalize on these changes than we are. Again, one prime, although painful, example is Japan.

The Japanese have undeniably proven that they are a manufacturing force to reckon with. The history books are loaded with industrial casualties due to their onslaught, for example, machine tools, consumer electronics, and personal computer hardware. From talks with many manufacturing professionals familiar with current practices in Japan and the United States, indications are that the gap is wider than most numerical evaluations reveal. Knowing what we now know about Japanese manufacturing techniques and practices, many feel we are five to ten years away from where they are today.

The Japanese fundamentally believe in and strive for continuous improvement. This is what drives their manufacturing organizations forward. It is the principle that they believe brought them to the point where they now are. There is no indication that they intend to stop doing what they think will eventually bring them to their goal, perfection.

On this basis it is clear that if we are ever going to catch up, we need to change at a rate that exceeds the rate of change of the Japanese. Failure to close the gap in productivity and quality cost will continue to yield global market share reductions and to erode the American standard of living.

A New School of Thought

American manufacturing companies also face increased competitive pressure from changes in management practices. One practice that is gaining in popularity is the reduction of suppliers. Companies are finding that there are several important benefits to be gained by reducing the number of suppliers with whom they do business. The practice is no longer even cutting-edge. World-class manufacturing companies have been paring down their supply bases for quite some time. The successes that both domestic and foreign manufacturers have had with these programs have been documented in virtually every major magazine and trade journal related to industry.

The logic behind the concept is so obvious that it is highly unlikely that it will turn around. From the purchasers' end, they can increase their influence with vendors. Supplier reduction will allow better communication to take place on a more frequent basis. It should also reduce the administrative support required within the buying organization in order to handle a larger supply network.

Many of the same benefits hold true for suppliers. They will be more closely connected to their respective customers. The result of this type of program is that fewer supplies are needed for each customer. Buying more parts from fewer people will put pressure on those suppliers to meet rigid requirements. The suppliers with less flexibility or narrower product range will look less attractive.

Many such programs are currently underway or in place at top performers. This means that better or more advanced companies will be in partnerships with the best suppliers. The longer either suppliers or customers wait to get going, the more likely it is that they will "partner up" with inferior performers. As this practice continues throughout the world, the competition to associate with good organizations will escalate.

Make versus Buy

One of the biggest debates in manufacturing over the years has been whether to make or buy components or services. No two organizations seem to share the same opinions on the issue. This question is one of those things that, like so many programs, comes and goes with management swings and magazine articles. The cause for the debate is rooted squarely in our accounting systems.

In most U.S. companies the make or buy decision on components or services is based on economic factors: "Is it cheaper to make or to purchase XYZ part?" is the most common, elemental form of a very sensitive question. For a company whose procurement or engineering functions are measured on cost, the decision appears cut-and-dried: all things being equal, go with the lower-priced option. The problem is that all things are never equal.

In manufacturing, the only thing that is predictable and constant is change. Many of the external variables with which manufacturing companies must deal are out of their control. It is widely proven that, in order to perform consistently at high quality and efficiency a process's variables must be under control. Given the fact that none of us can control what happens outside of our own environments (and few of us are successful at controlling even that), the make/buy issue becomes more complex. By focusing only on the cost of purchasing parts, we are being penny-wise and dollar-foolish. Studying the total cost to the organization of converting that component into final, saleable product is more to the point, though total cost is difficult to measure and therefore almost never captured.

The real question should be, "Which components and variables are critical to overall performance and cannot be jeopardized through the exposure of external influences?" Many companies have learned the hard way. They have sourced inexpensive components throughout the world only to find that their administrative requirements to handle those sources increase. They have had to increase inspection and re-work efforts, as well as paper-pushing efforts. Some of our clients have also seen inexpensive components turn into low-price subassemblies. These subassemblies turned into low-cost products that were sold into markets alongside their own products. Eventually, the client became little more than a distributor.

The most significant and real risk in third-party sourcing is that, over time, the technology for producing those critical components is lost. Once gone, the void that is created opens an organization up for several varieties of unpleasantness as a result of a weaker bargaining position and dependence on unattached sources.

Companies that are looking to get back in the driver's seat are now pulling more work in-house. They are finding that, although the price per unit may be lower outside, the control of total conversion costs and predictability in delivery and quality levels make them far and away better off. Many have realized that they still need the same amount of overhead to support key externally sourced supplies.

The impact of this trend toward vertical integration is a net reduction in the number of suppliers with whom a company will work. The further down the supply chain a company is from the end product, the more at risk it will be. As more companies start to realize the benefits of having greater control over production variables, vertical integration will continue to spread. This escalation will further heighten the competitive environment along the global supply chain.

Advances in communication and transportation have made the global market a reality. The level of sophistication of both consumers and producers continues to climb quickly. Even what were once considered to be Third World markets have ready access to, and understanding of, advanced technology. In this era of information, it is no longer acceptable or advisable to try to sell products or services with less than state-of-the-market features. Manufacturers must rise to world-class standards of comparison.

The first standard is lead time. How quickly can an organization deliver its products anywhere in the world and remain competitive with local sources? Customer requirements in most industry sectors are quickly decreasing from months to weeks. A perfect example is the machine tool industry where lead times were once quoted in seasons. Custom tool orders are now filled in a matter of weeks.

Market segmentation and demand swings will require factories to be capable of virtually instant response. These responses may be to model mix, volume changes, or design modifications. This will require linkages throughout the entire supply chain. Within that chain, each company will need to disseminate information to its organizations quickly and precisely. This type of flexible response will not be possible for traditionally organized and managed companies. Manufacturing organizations will have to be virtually flat, with autonomous, integrated work cells connected directly to upstream consumers. Traditionally structured hierarchy pyramids have been called the buggy whips of organizational structures.

The quality standard in the future will be measured in parts per million. For companies such as Motorola, the future is now. Motorola is producing communication equipment with fewer than six defective parts per million. The companies that are measuring quality in percentages are off the world-class mark by exponential factors! The world market leaders are designing products that are virtually impossible to produce with defects.

These changes in standards will impact the entire organization as it has evolved. It may very well require that we throw out every traditional rule of thumb, trade-off, or principle. Many of the managers who have gained the most from the existing structure stand to lose the most ground.

If this futuristic description of manufacturing seems incredible, it is. Too few U.S. manufacturing companies are prepared to deal with this scenario. Unfortunately, many aspects of this organizational and execution model are in place today at world-class companies. Companies are being forced to transform themselves into high-performance, world-class competitors. It is a traumatic and total change in how manufacturing companies are run. As Tom Peters says, "It is a world turned upside down." There are only two options for most manufacturers. The first and most difficult option is to accept what is happening and make the necessary changes. When history is written, it will record that most companies have taken the second option: to deny that they will need to change dramatically (or feel that the changes to be made are too difficult), and attempt to ride out the storm. This will no doubt be done in the hope that either their competitive environment will change or that, somehow, the clock will be turned back to when times were a little less complicated. Needless to say, time and opportunity wait for no one.

We have described the changes that have impacted the manufacturing world. These trends and events will continue to shape the competitive arena. They will continue to test the speed and agility of companies and management methods. In the next chapter, we address the strategies and tactics that leading global manufacturers are employing to succeed, rather than merely to survive.

Chapter 2

Strategies and Tactics
for Survival

Balancing the Subsystems

In the preceding chapter we discussed the inevitability of change. The companies that are first to come to grips with the competitive realities of today's manufacturing world will have a decided advantage over those that do not. Part of this realization is acknowledging that the market will drive the change effort. Those companies that have not yet significantly changed how they are organized and how they design and manufacture products are genuinely at risk. In fact, if you have not already made the modifications to your company that will allow maximum flexibility and speed in meeting world market demands, you may be too far behind to catch up. In all probability the company is riding the inertial momentum of historical market presence and performance, which, over time, will decay. The economic realities of the 1990s will force customers into alliances with suppliers that provide better value.

Up to now we have dealt with change in somewhat general terms. Change on a broad continuum will encompass many aspects of a manufacturing organization. It is difficult to pinpoint exactly which areas or functions of a company will be impacted by changes in the business environment. This is primarily due to the interdependencies of the subsystems and functions of every manufacturer, regardless of size.

Every manufacturing business has three main systems that it must manage:

- Technology system.
- People system.
- Business system.

Although we can discuss these as separate systems, they are intercon-

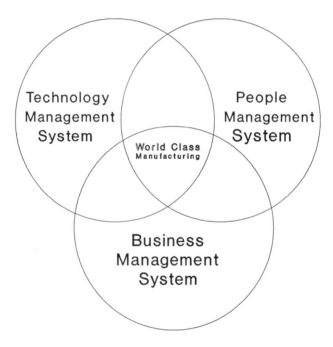

FIGURE 2.1.   The three key manufacturing systems.

SOURCE: Manufacturing Excellence Action Coalition, Simsbury, CT.

nected and overlap (see Figure 2.1). An event that impacts one system will have some effect on one or both of the other two systems. For example, new production technology introduced in the factory will require different skills in employees who operate the new equipment.

Technology Management Systems

Technology management systems are the provisions that assist the people in the organization. They allow the proper application of equipment, processes, and appropriate facilities to accomplish the goals and objectives outlined in the company's business plan. Examples of such systems would include manufacturing cells, computer-aided design and manufacturing equipment, materials requirement planning systems, and quick changeover machinery, as well as production lines. The systems help improve both the speed and the reliability with which people can perform their functions. The key to success is trying to *assist*, as opposed to displace, the people within the entire organization. If such systems yield productivity increases that result in job displacements, the respective program will be undermined by those employees responsible for its continued success.

Management is under pressure to find ways to absorb the increased productivity. Ways our clients have taken advantage of the increases in productivity include cross-training employees, whittling down backlog orders, accelerating new product introductions, and pursuing new market segments to increase sales volume. Failure to take advantage of the time thus freed up is a common mistake. The typical response is to lower head count. The message sent out by such action is very strong and very wrong: it will not take long before the rank and file close in to squelch the initiative.

People Management Systems

People management systems are those activities, practices, and procedures that will empower the company's people. They provide the direction and challenge in the development of people. These systems assist the employees in the application of available and affordable resources toward the achievement of the company's business plan. Included in such systems are employee education programs, focused involvement teams, and self-directed work groups. People management systems reduce the red tape typical of most traditional companies. They allow decision making to be leveraged and made at the lowest level that is realistically possible. In order to realize this tremendous benefit, people need to be armed with clear objectives and proper skill sets. Unfortunately, these requirements are not common in the classic pyramid type of organizational structure.

Business Management Systems

Business management systems are the company's practices, policies, and procedures. They plan and direct the activities of the organization's personnel in applying company resources to satisfy customer requirements. These systems include a company's compensation and reward system, organizational structure, distribution systems, and management of the supply chain. Business management systems are critical because no company has unlimited resources. The winners in manufacturing are those who understand how to maximize the amount of value they add while minimizing the resources they require to add this value. The most precious resource in today's manufacturing and business world in general is time.

Objectives of the Three Systems

Each of the three systems has an objective. The objective of the technology management system is to achieve a highly flexible production environment. This flexibility requirement is based on the continued propagation of market segments and technological innovation. People management systems need to provide the capability for rapid improvement and adaptation to change. Here, again, we must accept the fact that change is inevitable and that the speed with which the necessary modifications are made is the deciding factor in our survival. The objective of the business management system is to apply carefully the organization's limited resources, including capital and hard assets as well as time and human assets. Until quite recently, time and personnel were never managed with the same eye as hard assets. And although it was common to hear people say, "People are our most valuable asset," few companies actually managed as if this were true.

Integrating Principles

The three systems are integrated by principles that, in a sense, hold them together. These principles are meant to provide a framework to focus the direction in which companies that aspire to be world-class performers will need to head. They are:

- Total quality commitment.

- Respect for people.

- Short manufacturing cycles.

Figure 2.2 illustrates how these themes fit in with the three main manufacturing systems.

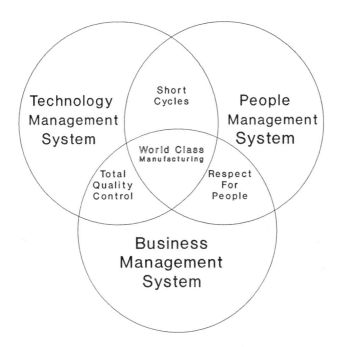

FIGURE 2.2.   Integrating principles for manufacturing systems.

Source: Manufacturing Excellence Action Coalition, Simsbury, CT.

The Need for World-Class Manufacturing

As economic borders fade, manufacturers will need to become "world-class." This will require the development of an operational approach that will achieve significant and continuous improvement in performance. It will demand the concentration of activities that add value to the product and the virtual elimination of waste. These world-class performers will successfully minimize both the time and the resources consumed within the total business cycle. The emphasis will be on tracking the time that elapses from spending cash to collecting cash. World-class manufacturing will require the continual improvement of total quality and productivity in all areas of the organization. Two key success factors will be speed and flexibility of response to any changes, be they internal or external to the company. Once the internal systems are in place and operational, the infrastructure has been developed. The remaining hurdle required to be considered a genuine world-class performer is the extension of these capabilities throughout the entire supplier base and customer network. The reason why we have put customers and suppliers last is that, without the understanding and discipline it takes to change yourself, you will be less capable of influencing and assisting external concerns.

Many valuable programs and good concepts have been tarnished because companies have attempted to implement concepts with only an elementary understanding of what is entailed. It is commonly the case that a larger customer requests that a supplier make some change that suits the customer's best interests. We frequently see, for example, companies demanding that suppliers use statistical process control to monitor the quality of the parts they supply. In many instances the request comes from a company that may not be using this technique (or, at least, not at the moment), but that understands how dandy it would be if its suppliers did. The ability of a typically smaller, unsophisticated supplier to implement such a mechanism is greatly reduced if its "partner" cannot offer some assistance. By "assistance," we mean financial or consulting support, as opposed to spiritual and moral support for another "good idea."

A second example of how imposed programs or edicts hurt legitimate causes is the experience some companies have had with Just-In-Time (JIT). In the classic scenario, a company becomes enlightened to the fact that it would be better served if it had less inventory. As this American tale commonly goes, the manufacturing group is directed to "do it" and the materials and/or purchasing group is directed to go out to the suppliers and "make it happen." The procurement people then charge out and inform the vendors, on whom they invariably have the most influence, to do three things: first, they are expected to ship parts in lower quantities with more frequent deliveries; second, they must do this with forecasts and schedules that are still subject to the normal fluctuations; and third, since this is a business partnership, the price of the material is not subject to change. No doubt some readers may be smiling because they know this story. Is it any mystery that many companies have been turned off by JIT? Somehow it has seemed okay to make these types of demands on our supply networks without the discipline to put the concepts in place within our own organizations.

World-Class Strategies

One of the benefits of being in the consulting field is that it allows one the opportunity to work with and study a large cross-section of companies and industries around the world. This exposure allows us to investigate what makes various manufacturing businesses successful.

We have the chance to see these operations from both inside and out. In so doing, one can't avoid seeing threads of commonality among the really outstanding companies. What we have found is that, regardless of size, industry, or geographical location, there appear to be five principles that stick out in the companies perceived to be "world-class." In this case, world-class companies are defined as those that so completely and consistently provide their customers satisfaction that they can charge a premium for their products and continue to enjoy greater customer loyalty and profits than their competition can do. It is impossible to place hard figures on the concept of world-class. Each company in every industrial sector is different. The situation is further compounded because there is no point at which a company passes some benchmark approval. The performance required to keep up in a global competition continues to move into further stages of refinement as the upper limits are shattered by the leader.

If achieving the level of performance of your particular segment's leader will require several years of transition, then unless the leader's progress halts you may never catch up. If this seems ominous, it should. The days are numbered for any company that is not already involved in a major campaign to adopt the proven principles of contemporary manufacturing.

You are a candidate for extinction if:

- Management is still deciding what type of quality program is right for you.
- The company is organized by functional departments according to a traditional pryamid structure.
- The organizational mindset is to maximize efficiency by dedicating specialists to tasks and leveraging quantities using economies of scale.
- Management is seeking to reduce direct labor hours through technological breakthroughs in hardware or software to eliminate "human factors."
- The company insists that vendors must supply defect-free materials, on time, with price a secondary concern—and then uses dollars to measure the effectiveness of its own purchasing department.
- You believe that going out for competitive bids on purchased materials is the way to keep your supply "partners" honest.

The organizations that we find struggling to make it or wallowing in mediocre performance share the traits listed above. They are the groups whose names will go into the history books to be reflected upon nostalgically by tommorrow's generation of manufacturers.

On the other hand, the companies that are today benefiting from what appears to be a chaotic time for markets and industries have certain strategies in common. They all currently demonstrate:

- Total quality commitment.
- Simplified value conversion methods.
- Production flexibility.
- Effective judgment through employee involvement.
- Strong supply chain networks.

To clarify each strategy or principle, we will take a closer look into how they are being applied. We will also expand on the foundation and composition of each strategy as it applies generally to all manufacturers and in particular as it relates back to the role of the people.

Total Quality Commitment

True quality commitment requires a never-ending obsession with and dedication to the delivery of customer satisfaction by everyone in the organization. There are three main areas that must be balanced in order to begin the application of quality as a strategy. From the business aspect, the company must be able to identify and design a superior product based on customer input and values. The technological aspect requires a superior method of aligning the organization's structures and systems to produce these products. The human side of the strategy requires superior people to ensure and support the first two. All three aspects are requisite for successfully achieving world-class quality.

There was a day, once upon a time, when quality was an avenue to differentiate a product or company from its competitive field. Typically, the "quality" product was easy to pick out because it came with the highest cost. In the United States especially, high quality and high price became synonymous. It was generally accepted that not only was this relationship true, but that it was proportional. Americans seemed truly to believe that the higher the quality we needed, the more that product was going to cost. This thinking was used as a foundation for companies to develop entire marketing campaigns and business plans. Eventually the actual cost to produce these products escalated. No matter to be concerned about, however, because the increase in cost can be passed right along to the customer. Suddenly, however, there came a shock that stunned those who managed by this rule.

Competition started to heat up and customers started to have more options from which to choose. Many companies found it unbelievable that quality might not necessarily have to be more expensive. At first, it took a while for customers to let go of the quality versus cost trade-off. Those days are gone. Many of the manufacturers that refused to believe that quality and cost were not synonymous are gone as well. We still come across (for now, anyway) organizations fighting to let this one go.

We see manufacturing management often falling into a conventional-wisdom trap. The trap is opened with the desire to improve quality. What most organizations do is check everything a little closer and a little more carefully. In so doing, inspection is invariably overloaded. The pressure starts to mount as things sit waiting to be inspected and shipments start to lag. The pressure increases to the point where defects start to slip by because of rushed work paces. There is never enough time to identify and fix the causes of the defects that are found. The lack of root cause problem resolution ensures that the problem will reoccur. Coupled with Murphy's Law (which, by the way, reached its peak in manufacturing), it ensures that the problem will resurface at the worst possible time.

In order to break free from this trap one must realize several truths. The first is that quality is the *result* of several activities, it is not the screened residual of a process. It is the result of dedicated people making producible designs using reliable and predictable processes. Quality is not something that gets inspected in at the conclusion of a series of randomly variable events.

To achieve quality levels that can be considered world-class, companies must understand the role each function needs to play. First and foremost, there needs to be a commitment to quality throughout management. This will require a genuine understanding of the quality concept, and its appreciation. The management ranks will need to demonstrate their dedication and leadership to the rest of the organization and to the world. By "demonstrate," we mean making some tough decisions and then standing by them. During the course of our consulting practice it is rare to find a management group that does not profess to know what quality is all about. But it is even more rare to find an organization that won't make compromises or trade-offs to save money or face, especially at the end of the month or quarter. It is these seemingly small "exceptions" that undermine the credibility and longevity of most quality programs. Overstepping the boundary, even once, sends powerful signals absorbed by employees and customers. When it comes down to dollars and cents—and at some point it always does—this is when true dedication and leadership are put to the test. Over the past few years American management has often shown only that talk is still cheap.

There must be commitment to quality in the product's design and delivery. It is amazing and, in a way, embarrassing that only quite recently has the concept of design for manufacturability been given much attention in the United States. If you were to poll the engineering and design people within your organization, how many would you find who have spent significant time in actual manufacturing operations? Because of the functional structure of companies and vertical progression of employees, most organizations have few if any design engineers with nut-and-bolt manufacturing experience. To make matters worse, manufacturing is usually the last group to see new designs. By that stage in the game, 70 percent of the cost of the product has been cast. The burden of cost reductions and quality attainment, however, continues to rest on manufacturing.

How can the quality of a product's design be gauged? There are some general principles that assist in evaluating design quality. One principle is manufacturability. Is the product planned, designed, and introduced within a predetermined and known process capability to result in the lowest possible total cost? The concept of manufacturability requires that quality assurance systems exist in each stage of the product's development. It holds that predetermined stages and milestones are checked and accepted within the time specified. If these concepts are properly applied, there should be no need for major changes after the release of the product and the cost should decline along a normal learning curve.

The second principle in design quality has to do with a concept relating to the acceptability of output in each phase to the person or group relying on that output to perform their function. Along the entire chain of events each person must consider himself a company. They have an obligation to their customer, who is the next person or group in the chain. The producer is responsible for assuring that the product meets the customer's need. Success is determined when there is a definite uninterrupted, connected, and continuous flow through the process. At each step, feedback and resolution of problems are treated with a sense of urgency. The identification of potential process improvements becomes evident and is exploited. The final element is for the design process to become both highly reliable and self-regulating.

To be successful, the various players will need to be able to communicate effectively with each other. This will require the modification of traditional reporting relationships to produce an integrated effort.

Only with a cross-functional group can all aspects of the process be addressed early enough to ensure high quality and affordability. The changes that must take place in order to organize this way will require proactive leadership and managerial dedication.

In addition to quality designs, total quality is dependent on the production process. It reflects the reliability, responsiveness, and flexibility of the systems employed. Of these aspects, the most significant is reliability. Process reliability and predictability are the cornerstones of quality. World-class performers painstakingly study their processes and systems. They develop the control systems that virtually prohibit new or unknown variables from impacting their processes.

Think of developing a scientific experiment. Looking back on your high school or college lab days, you will probably recall how precisely each step had to be performed in order to yield the correct result. Once the required equipment and materials identified were in working order, the experiment could be repeated at will. The pain was not in performing the steps themselves. The tough part lay in not missing any steps or misreading a measurement.

The same principles hold true in manufacturing. At first blush, there appear to be an infinite number of variables that come into play on even a simple product. Most companies have never actively tried to eliminate or reduce the variables they control. By not analyzing the process, by widening specifications and allowing the process to be performed differently each time, we ensure that the result will be poor quality. Up to now our policy has been to sift through and pick out the nonconforming results in the belief that they were the exceptions to the norm. In actuality, the less precise and less accurate the process and specifications are, the greater the range of results will be. The wider the range of results, the more "normal" defects will become. The key to high production quality is knowing the process capability and how variation introduced anywhere in the cycle will affect the outcome. Merely tracking the results of a process will never bring you up to world-class quality performance.

Total quality must be a commitment by the people producing the product. Our experience has shown that management has been quick to point out the enormous influence the workers have on product quality, and how by "paying a little more attention" to what they were doing, they could boost quality figures dramatically. Without any doubt, there is some truth to this complaint. Since the people who touch the process last also typically have the least political clout in the organization, who better to blame? What we have found is that the commitment of the workforce to quality is a reflection of the commitment of management.

Regardless of what country you travel to, there seems to be spirit and some commonalities on the factory floor. It is always a place where action speaks louder than words. On the floor it is always obvious what a company's commitment to quality and opinion of the workers really are like. In the manufacturing plant, this commitment is reflected in the state of cleanliness and organization. There is no place that better demonstrates that "a picture is worth a thousand words" than the shop floor.

Manufacturers deemed to be world-class are succeeding in developing the competence, morale, and quality consciousness along with a spirit of improvement in their workforce. They are dedicating the resources required in education as well as in tooling and equipment. These organizations lead by example and devote tremendous energy to understanding their people, in addition to the process systems themselves. Companies have found that they can extract extraordinary performance and quality from quite ordinary people. It is the improvement of the workforce in conjunction with that of the product design and production process that will allow achievement of the highest quality levels.

Simplified Value Adding

Top performing manufacturing companies continuously focus on their total conversion cycle time. The cycle begins with a commitment of resources and ends when cash is collected from a satisfied customer. Our definition of cycle encompasses more than the production itself. The ability to accelerate the total end-to-end time is a significant factor in determining overall productivity and competitiveness. By isolating the flow of information and work required to complete the entire cycle, the process can be studied and simplified. World-class companies pay close attention to both the number of steps and the amount of time it takes to go from first inquiries to revenue collection.

Within the conversion cycle, there are two types of activities that take place:

- Those that add value to the product.
- Those that add cost.

Either activity type takes time. Invariably, the longer it takes, the more it costs. We are sure that this isn't a shocking revelation to anyone. But who actually manages on a basis of how long an activity takes or how many steps are involved in executing an order? The real shock occurs when we lead managers through an exercise of charting the steps involved from order receipt to product shipment. The exercise is an enlightening one if, when completed, it includes all actual details.

Typical American companies are organized by function. Each function is given neat boundaries around its responsibilities. These functional kingdoms have their own hierarchies and agendas. The people of each of these kingdoms have limited exposure to, or understanding of, how their day-to-day activities affect the business as a whole. For example, a clerk in the order entry functional department may know very little about how production control or manufacturing uses the information she or he provides. How could they be expected to know based on the amount of time they typically spend with the other functions within the same company (usually none) or directly communicating with them (minimal, if any)? We find that the larger the company is, the greater the isolation of functional departments and personnel. To make the problem even worse, in the largest organizations the kingdoms are located in different buildings, states, or sometimes even in different countries.

For many years, management at the most senior level believed that if each department or function was doing well, then the company would, by default, do well. "Doing well" meant that the function was "effectively" managed, operated within budget, and performed its duties as described in the corporate grand scheme. The kingdom's manager measured his or her political power based on the size of the kingdom. Quite often these managers felt their primary duties were to protect and defend the population from attack from outside (another department). Losing sight of who the real enemies were, departments and functions fought each other.

Senior management emphasized the system by directing functional leadership to maximize the efficiency of their respective departments. This push created imbalances within the company that caused bottlenecks in the overall process. Conflicts and tensions arose between functions. Finger pointing and bad blood between functionally dependent departments brought afflictions to what were healthy companies. The most pronounced symptom was the virtual breakdown of cooperation and communication essential to long-term survival: the "Us versus Them" sentiment is prevalent in many companies today.

It is quite common for marketing and manufacturing to have an antagonistic relationship. Manufacturing gets upset because marketing is unable to forecast demand or constantly changes requests. The quality department is sure that no one in operations cares about quality. Operations is convinced that quality inspectors deliberately search for something wrong with products. Engineering is positive that no one else in the organization understands the products as well as they do. Sales gives products away and makes promises no one can keep. Distribution never has the right products on the shelf. We could go on and on, but the point should be clear.

The truth is that each functional stereotype has some thread of validity. But because of the way our people are organized, they never truly understand what goes on in other areas of the company. Myths and stereotypes are adopted as realities, and groups learn how to avoid dealing with one another directly. This becomes easy to do when the rival faction is on another floor or in another facility.

A classic example of what we are discussing occurred at Xerox. Xerox was one of America's sweetheart companies. It invented the process of xerography used to photocopy documents. It was a traditionally organized company with an admirable history. Xerox believed that they were the center of wisdom in the industry. But in the 1980s something started to sour.

Xerox started to gain a very clear understanding of what global competition was all about. It saw its market share start to fade and profits plummet. Xerox had lost significant market share and millions of dollars in profit in a single year. The staggering reality was dramatized when Xerox found out its competitors were selling machines for less than what it cost Xerox to produce them. According to one V.P. of engineering, Xerox was mystified because from a department-to-department standpoint, each function was doing fine. But the company was clearly going down the tubes.

Xerox undertook a comprehensive effort to benchmark what its competitors were doing. It was difficult to admit that they could possibly learn something from someone else, but by studying the practices of its world-class competitors, Xerox began to identify opportunities to improve their products and processes to regain lost market share. Fundamental to the changes were the identification and elimination of the real cost drivers of the company.

We have found, during the course of our practice, that the companies that have felt a shock or are in discomfort are the most successful at implementing the type of changes required by today's manufacturing environment. Many of the changes require a rethinking of the entire structural model of most American companies. Without some degree of pain, few management groups are willing to bite the bullet and take the necessary actions. Unfortunately, the longer they wait, the greater the competitive gap will be and the less likely it is that they will be able to recover.

The inefficiencies that are built into our existing systems will produce wastes that will accumulate over time and cause the eventual death of the company. By seeking to maximize the efficiency of discrete functions through independently automated systems, we will actually accelerate the organizational decay. Automation is only a benefit if the process being automated has been simplified. If it has not, then the result will be the automation of all inefficiencies within the system.

The American practice has been to slap a computer or robot on a department or function to speed it up. Then, as we speed up these functions, we hope to link them together via some network. Our hope is to manage technically around the way we are organized now. By putting enough money and gadgetry into our organization, we can avoid having to make really significant changes in our framework. Automated storage and retrieval systems (ASRSs) are a wonderful example of the technological capability we have developed to manage large amounts of inventory. They avoid the basic inability of management to control inventory by having a high tech place to put it. The

ASRS simplifies the accounting of material despite the proven fact that inventory is a liability to flexible production, and *not* an asset. The proliferation of these systems throughout the United States clearly shows our mindset. It is easier to pay for a technical toy than it is to address the root cause of why the toy seems necessary. Is it a mere coincidence that in Japan these systems are typically only used to queue finished products waiting for export ships?

On one level, management thinking was correct. It sought to reduce the time required within each function. Even in the absence of a co-ordinated effort, the total cycle time is minimally improved. But the most significant benefit is in the acceleration of the process itself. It requires the understanding of each functional role and activity incorporated in delivery of customer satisfaction. Most companies do not have a comprehensive plan for actually managing this complete cycle. Few manufacturing companies have the process documented in any form. It is only after the process is documented and confirmed to be accurate by each function that it can be evaluated.

We cannot overemphasize the importance of mapping out this process. Most managers believe they know how their company works. It has been our experience that in every case where we attempted this, no one person has been able to map the total cycle completely. Consider improving efficiency a journey: before you embark on the journey you must have directions. In order for the directions to be developed, your guide must know where you are starting. Without this starting point, any vehicle, at any speed, in any direction you choose may not get you any closer to where you want to go.

The goal of simplification is to concentrate on the activities that add value to the customer's product. In so doing, the waste of the cycle is purged. The additional benefit is that people can more easily deal with a less complicated process. The less complex the cycle, the less likely it is to be fouled up and the less time it will take. We have found that the people who deal with the existing systems are both the most knowledgeable and the most willing to help simplify them. The challenge rests with management's ability to organize, coordinate, and execute a plan that leads to the continuous flow of work throughout the entire company.

Production Flexibility

In today's manufacturing environment, customers are more knowledgeable and sophisticated than ever. There once was a time when quality could be used as a means to differentiate a company from its competitors. This is no longer the case. High quality is the minimum expected from every company. Once companies are sufficient, by global standards, in quality, they can pursue production flexibility as strategy.

Manufacturing companies will seek to differentiate themselves on the basis of how quickly they can react to new customer demands. These demands may affect:

• Schedules.

• Engineering and/or design changes.

• New product introductions.

Both high quality and affordability will be givens. Markets are volatile and will continue the trend of wanting increased product variety and shorter lead times. Companies that wrestle with quality issues or manage by conventional rules will require lots of inventory to cope. Inventory will be the tax paid, levied in time and money, in direct proportion to an organization's inefficiency. As the competition forces manufacturers to become more financially efficient, the tax will eventually devastate them.

The survivors will be the companies that can achieve the flexibility their markets demand with minimal inventory.

A company's flexibility is dependent on several variables. Each aspect of overall flexibility is measured in time. The lead time to make the necessary change determines how flexible the organization is in regard to that modification.

The companies that are making strides in their flexibility are addressing:

• Total cycle time in the factory.

• Supplier lead times.

• Customer lead times (including change orders and order entry).

- Processing engineering changes.
- Tooling and equipment reaction time.
- Process and equipment changes in the plant.

By "addressing," we mean *actively managing* the activities that are taking place in the various functional offices as well as in the factory. This involves understanding how time is being spent along the process in a detailed and comprehensive manner. Let's take a closer look at some of the areas we have listed.

Total cycle time in the factory

We have worked with and met manufacturing professionals from across the country during the course of our practice. We also attend and present at numerous conventions and seminars attended by industry professionals and other consultants. We have seen that the definition and interpretation of terms often vary from one organization to another. This is particularly the case with the term "cycle time." We would like to offer a definition of cycle time.

Cycle time is the time that it takes for materials to go from the first activity in receiving completely through the final shipping process. For example, if a stopwatch was attached to a component in receiving upon receipt, cycle time would be the elapsed time until the shipping container was sealed. Several things impact cycle time using this definition, including:

- Moving materials.
- Counting parts.
- Inspecting components.
- Staging batches.
- Conversion operations.
- Storage.
- Consumption velocity.

The point we want to stress is that once the clock starts, time continues to accumulate. The cycle time is not just the sum of all "work time" to produce a part, or the frequency at which parts get pumped out of the system. By our definition, cycle time includes all the time parts sit waiting for the next activity. Evaluating cycle time this way, we typically find that 90 percent to 95 percent of the time material is in house and "in process," nothing is happening to it. In order to become more flexible, companies must focus on the root causes of the delays in the complete cycle.

A major factor in long cycle times (and therefore poor flexibility) is batch size. The logic is quite simple: let's say our company makes model As and model Bs in batches of 1,000. We run As first and then run Bs. We ship every five days in batches of 1,000. The B parts are delivered to the floor on the day the line was planned to finish the run of As. But, as usual, we are behind schedule on As by one day. The set of 1,000 parts for Bs sits and waits until #1,000 A is completed. The cycle for model B includes this delay, plus the five days required to get to the thousandth B, or six days. A new customer wanting a model A will have to wait until all model Bs are done and the next run of 1,000 As is finished before they are available.

Most domestic manufacturers buy materials in batches, move parts in batches, run operations through a batch, move the batch to the next operation, and so on, and the way in which most manufacturers are organized to produce products makes batches necessary. Large batches of inventory are insurance in many plants. The insurance is there to cover shortcomings in planning and executing. Having "a little extra" is required when you are unable to know accurately how much of what goes where and when. It is vital in keeping production going if quality becomes a significant problem. Excessive trips between departments and operations can be reduced by increasing batch sizes. Because of long setup times on equipment, a big batch helps make changeover more economical.

To be competitive, manufacturing people have got to change the mindset that sees batches as necessary. They must attack whatever was the justification for processing work in batches. Reducing batches reduces the largest waste in manufacturing: time. The goal is to have material flow directly from one operation to the next with little or no waiting.

Let's take a closer look at what drives the need to have batches.

The first place to look is within the sales department. The chances are quite good that there are policies that encourage customers to buy big batches, for example, policies that grant discounts for large-quantity buys. Another example might be charging customers extra for multiple shipments against an order. The typical rationale is that the supplier will run the entire order and incur additional storage costs. Part of the incremental charge is for the additional administrative paperwork and effort that are necessary to handle the order. Based on how the company is organized, the "specials" (small orders) will require multitudes of signatures and approvals. A third incentive for large batch orders is a policy of charging penalties to customers who do schedule multiple releases, but then change dates or quantities. This is typically easy money since customers inevitably change their own internal schedule to meet their customers' demands. These policies and practices help ensure that demand comes in lumps and bumps, which is perfect since we schedule big bunch runs.

The schedulers now do *their* thing: schedule batches of materials to support the demand lumps. They tweak and adjust the required batches a little higher to compensate for miscounts or possible quality problems. Depending on the part or department, they may also hedge by scheduling the order early. The parts that need to be machined will be rounded up to the "economical run size" determined primarily by the setup time. The orders then hit the floor.

The department foremen and supervisors juggle the orders based on capacity availability and manpower. The "normal" condition will inevitably result in jobs contending for limited resource capacity. These can usually be made up through overtime. To avoid future contention, however, the floor will run extra parts and keep them in storage for next time. Hopefully, if they run a big enough batch, they won't need to run them again for a while. Material consumption changes in spurts as large batches move from operation to operation.

The material group hedges against stockouts by having plenty of material on hand early. Materials and purchasing work together to batch-order their requirements. This way, they can save the company money by purchasing in volumes that make them eligible for quantity discounts. By taking the orders in one shot, they also reduce the required paperwork associated with generating and maintaining purchase orders. They also cut the transportation costs of multiple receipts by using big trailers.

Most manufacturing managers know that the majority of the workers are just out to milk the company. In order to avoid that, they give their people plenty of work to earn their keep. The parts they make will be needed, eventually.

The workforce, on the other hand, knows that their foremen are slave drivers. But since they need their jobs, they are more concerned with job security. To many, having plenty of work in front of them translates to need and, therefore, security.

Senior management is happy to see the plant hustling, machines whirling, and people working. Accounting is satisfied that enough standard hours are being generated to absorb the company overhead. Plant management is content to ship on budget each month (50 percent to 75 percent the last week) and maintains a healthy backlog of orders.

We hope you get the gist of what's wrong. Each function is attempting to do what is best for the company. They try to compensate for the perceived plans of other functions. Many American manufacturers have institutionalized the systems that demand building in batches. The batches hobble unevenly through the plant in spurts and sputters. Inventory gradually builds and provides the insurance without which many shops could not get by.

World-class companies recognize that batch processing can lead to inventory, and inventory is the shadow of inefficiency. Most are laid out to facilitate flow and eliminate time in queues, which always improves production flexibility.

Effective Employee Involvement

In today's competitive world, no company can afford to waste resources. The most underutilized resource of most manufacturing companies is their people. The companies that develop and leverage the capabilities of all their employees will achieve better performance than those that do not. The companies that fail to unlock the potential of their workforce will be forced to carry more overhead, have more layers of management, and will be slower to react.

Technologically, we have the ability to develop automated and unattended factories and warehouses. The cost, however, of this technology is as fantastic as its concept. For many organizations the price will be out of range. In the meantime, organizations are still going to need human beings to function. The men and women at every level of your company will determine the quality, flexibility, and performance of the organization. Competitors can duplicate equipment used, copy or license designs, or otherwise replicate products or processes. But competitors have no way of matching a company's workforce. As a unit, the workforce is a unique combination of individual members. It is impossible to duplicate without each individual component. Used to its full capability, the workforce is genuinely a competitive advantage.

With guidance and training, people's judgment can appreciate. Their mental flexibility is the asset and the manageable resource. Unfortunately, direct laborers have been conditioned over the years to check out mentally, as they punch in physically at the time clock. The reason so many shop workers look removed and disinterested in their work is that they are. People are products of their environment and it is management that creates the environment. The real obstacle to producing higher-quality products more efficiently is management, not the worker. W. Edwards Deming insists that management is 90 percent of the problem.

What we must understand is that we slid gradually into the position in which we now find ourselves. Factories don't start out dirty. Companies are not born with volumes of policies and tremendous bureaucracies. Manufacturing startups do not have large hierarchies and employee class systems. Each of these takes time to develop. All of these factors lead to low morale, tension, and conflicts between various factions, and to communication breakdowns. It is the erosion of a company's communication infrastructure that causes the quality and productivity problems that will render it noncompetitive at best.

More and more manufacturers are realizing that minds, are in fact, a terrible thing to waste. Companies like Hewlett-Packard, Northern Telecom, Digital Equipment Corporation, and NUMMI are seeing tremendous benefits from managing their human assets better. Outside the manufacturing sector, companies like Federal Express and Domino's absolutely rely on the involvement of their people to stay alive in brutally competitive businesses.

In order to utilize people more effectively, companies are going to have to make changes. In our experience, the first change required is also the most difficult for management to make: management must accept and demonstrate a new attitude, one in which workers are important as human beings. Management must believe that employees have a high degree of ability. They must provide the forum for people to demonstrate their full capabilities. And, finally, management must recognize that workers want to do a good job.

We cannot stress enough the importance (and difficulty) of retrofitting management's mindset. There will be times, especially in the beginning, when the workers will test management's faith. Infidelity in the management ranks will defeat the entire initiative and will often reverse any progress. At this point, the project is ready for the graveyard—the bookcase in the office that holds the other good ideas that have come and gone.

But let's say that management becomes enlightened to the operating realities of the 1990s. What will be required to achieve the flexibility and performance in the workforce to become world-class? We believe it will take the following:

- Broad-based employee involvement.
- Teams.
- Education and training.
- Appropriate recognition and reward systems.
- Simplified organizational structure.
- Elimination of archaic bureaucratic rules.
- Elimination of embarrassing conditions.

Broad-based employee involvement

Before the workforce can be a source of help or innovation, they need to understand why the company is changing its mode of operation and how they will fit in with the changes proposed. A mistake we commonly see is that management takes for granted that the people understand the business reason behind change. Change is difficult for most human beings. Resistance to change can be reduced somewhat if we take the time to communicate the fundamental reasons for it.

Communication and transmission are often confused. Communication requires sending a signal, which is then received and acknowledged by the receiver. It requires something be sent and received. Transmission, on the other hand, involves only sending a signal. Typically, we find that organizations *transmit* information to their people, as opposed to engaging in two-way communication.

Once the workforce understands the company's purpose, its involvement in the process can begin. The people will need some broad but guided direction that will focus their efforts on improvement activities. This will not work if people are turned loose to go after any initiative they believe worthy. As strange as this may seem, it is common for management groups to back off too far and let people decide for themselves on the projects. The sentiment is that, as long as things get "fixed," we are moving in the right direction. Unfortunately, one group's problem solution may not benefit the company as a whole. Time and effort are spent on problems that may be trivial in contrast to other, more primary opportunities. The role of management is to provide direction and not directives. To avoid an approach that is myopic, the involvement groups and project focus need balance. This balance can be achieved by having representatives from a broad cross-section of the organization looking at a problem affecting a wide range of functions.

Teams

The team concept provides the framework through which employees can best become involved. The purpose of having a cross-functional team is not to mend fences between functional groups, it is to tear them down. There is no better way to collapse the time required to produce or process anything than by integrating the events that are needed to make it happen. Combining the people and processes increases the volume and speed of communications, which improves response time. The result is faster problem resolution and better flexibility.

There are numerous examples of teams, in place today, delivering unprecedented results. Perhaps the most widely publicized was Ford Motor Company's team Taurus. The team is credited with the complete development of the Ford Taurus. For Ford, it was a significant bet on the team concept. The team's achievement has been given credit for helping Ford's resurgence in the marketplace. The achievements of other teams in a wide variety of industries prove the validity of the concept. The approach has been heralded in virtually every trade and industrial magazine published. The question becomes how long before you get on with it or must compete against it.

Education

Education is the cornerstone of success in maximizing employee involvement and the team approach. This is an area in which we are deficient in the United States. The United States is considered the melting pot of the world. A closer look actually reveals more of a tossed salad than a melted homogeneous society. Companies are starting to realize that the players on the teams they hope to field may literally not be able to talk to one another. A client we worked with recently had a team of thirty-six people who spoke ten different languages. Having English as a common denominator was a long-term goal. Our point is that senior management must realize that merely physically or functionally linking people together doesn't produce a team.

The first issue many factories in the United States are going to have to deal with is identifying the skill set of the workforce. The skills will be both technical and nontechnical. Nontechnical skills include English literacy, interpersonal and social demeanor, and tolerance for change. Technical skills include math capabilities, problem-solving skills, and other job-specific technical skills (reading prints, equipment setup and maintenance, statistical process control, etc.). The education and training requirements for the workforce can be developed to provide the skills necessary to work effectively in teams.

Recognition and reward systems

Recognition and reward are not synonyms. Recognition is the public acknowledgment for a job well done or for an honest attempt at a worthwhile cause. This can vary from a pat on the back to reports in a company newsletter to testimonial dinners. Every human being has an ego. Granted, some are larger and some more modest. Recognition systems serve to stroke the ego. When sincere and equitably done, they return significantly more than the required investment. But, as important as recognition is, it doesn't pay the bills.

The reward and compensation systems of any company must be fair and equitable. They should reflect the responsibilities of the people performing the necessary tasks. We will talk at length about some appropriate reward systems in Chapters 5 and 6.

Simplified organizational structure

Among the most significant benefits of involving the workforce through team-based activity is the reduction in technical and supervisory support required on the floor. This is most effectively accomplished through the utilization of self-directed work teams. Such work teams have gone so far as to assume personnel and administrative duties as well. These tremendous benefits can only be realized if:

- The people are educated to the point where the support functions are no longer required; and
- management is willing to relinquish the power and authority to the employee teams.

Problems typically arise when employee teams get charged up to act on an opportunity and then are not given the time to work on it. This may occur when each team member still reports to a departmental "boss" who has other crises for that member to address. When a team operates within the confines of a traditional structure, the team members have conflicting allegiances. This conflict has caused the paralysis and eventual death of many teams.

Organizational structures and reporting relationships must be modified to support a team-based workforce. Executed correctly, the changes result in fewer organizational layers, as required in productive, fast-paced organizations.

Archaic rules

Rest assured that any organization that has been around a while follows some bureaucratic dogma. Formally, the policies and rules are spelled out in black and white. Informally, this is "the way we do things around here." Either form of dogma serves to control and govern the chain of command. The majority of this legislation was written to cover someone's rear. Any policy or practice that restricts the flexibility or the speed at which events take place must be eliminated or changed because such rigidity runs counter to developing a world-class manufacturing culture.

Embarrassing conditions

American management is quite keen on the concept of teams. But are we prepared to take some of the good-faith steps toward team development? Many of these steps involve giving up perks and status barriers that have been erected over the years to separate "us" from "them."

We believe that the reason why managers and technical support people in the United States do not spend much time in the factory is because the factory is very likely a dump. Factories that are dirty, dark, and depressing are more the rule than the exception. The disparity between the work environments in the office and in the shop should humiliate most management staffs. This provides a clear signal to the entire workforce as to which group of folks rate and which ones are second-class.

We regularly encounter hundreds of examples of embarrassing conditions and policies. Classic cases include reserved parking, separate dining facilities, punching time clocks, and labor grade assignments. Until many of the blatantly obvious inequities are removed, how can people rally in support of teams and the company?

Strong Supply Chain

No company stands alone in this world. Every organization, be it manufacturer or otherwise, is dependent on both customers and suppliers. How well a company manages both of these external concerns will ultimately determine how successful that company will be. For the sake of discussion, we will assume that the company's internal affairs are operating effectively and under control. Whether customers or suppliers are more important is irrelevant since without both, there is no business. As elementary as this might seem, there are few manufacturing companies that share the same management concern, effort, and sense of urgency in both of these relationships. Survival in the 1990s will mandate that both networks be managed with the same intensity.

Our friends in the computer world are guided by a fundamental truth: "garbage in equals garbage out." Obviously the same holds true in manufacturing. We have been focusing on how to keep the garbage from getting in. Suppliers have been using inspection and QC to sift out bad product, and customers have been checking the product again as it comes in. As long as both sides have to keep sifting through piles of product, both sides have to keep extra piles around to make sure there is enough good stuff to keep them going. Both sides keep looking and sure enough, both find some defects. The more defects they find, the greater the number and size of the piles they have to keep and the longer it takes to look at them. As the amount of inventory goes up, the operating costs go up and overall flexibility goes down.

Operating costs increase with the amount of inventory because inventory requires:

- More receipt transactions.
- More freight.
- More counting.
- More inspection.
- More moves.
- More warehouse.
- More people to do all the above.

All of these, in addition to the purchase price, consume capital—capital that is now unavailable to invest in new opportunities as they arise.

Successful manufacturing companies demonstrate the ability to be highly responsive. The most profitable ones can do so with very little inventory. In order for this to occur, world-class companies develop highly responsive and cooperative efforts with suppliers as well as customers. The goal in developing and strengthening this network is to foster synergistic opportunities for mutual business benefits.

To be effective, the network must be organized to minimize the communication and transactional costs while accelerating the velocity of change. The transactional costs include all of the administration ceremonies we perform now. They include the development and issue of purchase orders, tit-for-tat price bickering, outgoing and incoming inspections, and a myriad of other activities. Each step adds cost rather than value to the process. The real penalty is the accumulation and loss of time. Once again, time is the key measurement and focal point.

Management must understand that genuine commitment to a supplier relationship will yield the lowest total cost. The lowest total cost is realized by focusing on critical nonprice areas. These areas are the true cost drivers. The emphasis of the supply base must be on:

- Total quality focus.
- Response time to change.
- Reliability.
- Total cost driven.

We would like to point out a few things about commitment. Committed customers do not abandon you for slightly lower prices. They do not succumb to penetration tactics by alternate suppliers. Partners do not use strong-arm tactics to put the squeeze on suppliers, especially smaller ones. On the other hand, committed suppliers do not send defective products, or miss deliveries, or inflate prices.

Manufacturers must alter their Neanderthal approaches to procurement and adopt a more cooperative attitude. The first element, already touched on, is long-term commitment. Long-term is the life-cycle of the product a component goes into. The network needs to share quality information and goals as they relate to the process. Cooperation will require frequent communication of data and the involvement of diverse functional personnel. In advance-manufacturing supply-chain networks it is common for companies to share technical resources and design responsibility. Companies are finding tremendous advantages in utilizing supplier expertise during up-front product specification and development. Early supplier involvement has led to lower costs, higher quality, and better performance in new products.

The establishment of an effective supply network that is both highly cooperative and responsive will require the adoption of a new mind-set. There is a certain hesitancy on the part of many companies when they hear the term "partner" because this term has often been abused. Good suppliers have been approached by potential "partners" who express a desire to enter into more cooperative relationships. More often than not, the emphasis somehow reverts back to price concessions as a symbol of intent or good will. And as long as the purchasing functions are measured, within their own organizations, by dollars and budget variances, the song will stay the same.

The way in which the entire procurement function is organized, measured, and compensated must be aligned to support the broader company objectives. Its goal should be to formulate a program to attack the total costs and all non-value-adding activities with outside concerns. A major obstacle to the success of such a program is the large number of suppliers commonly found.

Establishing a commitment and gaining meaningful cooperation with a supplier are difficult and time-consuming. The greater the number of suppliers, the more enormous the task becomes. Having several suppliers for a given commodity also dilutes the overall effectiveness of the effort. Reducing the number of suppliers with which a company deals has several advantages.

First, it will immediately get some attention. Actions speak louder than words . . . and they move a lot faster too. By whittling down the number of vendors, both internal and external concerns will start taking notice. The first examples will give the program the initial political momentum it requires. The effort also naturally starts to reduce the scope of the overall task. Reductions in the total number of suppliers will lessen the various administrative burdens associated with each.

Second, it is illogical to think that a company can establish tight network bonds with several hundred or, for some companies, thousands of suppliers. Often, these relationships require the development of personal rapport. It takes time to foster the trust between the organizations. A good analogy is dating. Both people have their guard up at first and are on their best behavior. It takes a while to catch the other person without his or her game face on. The rites, rituals, and psychological games of dating are just like those of procurement. As human beings we are compelled to act on emotion and then justify our actions with some tailored logic. The way in which one approaches a marriage is typically quite different from the way one handles short-term liaisons.

Let's take a look at a real-life example. NCR produces business equipment and systems. They are in a highly competitive market with some formidable competitors. To make matters worse, NCR's customers have an expectation that each year the price will go down, not up! With upwards of 60 percent of their costs attributed to purchased materials, suppliers appeared as an attractive area for improvement. The first issue to surface in attempting to scope out the effort was that this particular plant had 600 suppliers. The company's efforts have been able to reduce that number to under 200. Thirty of these suppliers represented better than 80 percent of the purchased dollars. This strategic core of suppliers are the ones NCR targeted first.

The program sought to establish a closer bond between NCR and its suppliers and, in an effort to prove its sincerity, NCR entered into five-year agreements with certain vendors. In exchange it wanted more insight into how the suppliers were managing their internal processes. The point was not to squeeze the suppliers' margin, but rather to provide assistance in reducing the total process costs. In fact, as NCR became more dependent on key suppliers, it also was obligated to protect these suppliers' margins and viability. NCR was able to reach agreement on a fifty/fifty split to any savings they were able to identify in the supplier's operation. According to both camps, the program is building unprecedented cooperation in the achievement of a mutually beneficial business relationship.

There are other examples of companies making moves in the right direction. The best suppliers will be sought out by customers taking these steps first. This will leave the marginal many to those companies that are slower out of the starting blocks. Once again, the decided advantage will go to the players in your market who secure the capacity and commitment of the best suppliers in the industry.

Chapter **3**

The Productivity Programs

The previous two chapters looked at what has been going on in the manufacturing world. We shared some of the common elements that distinguish world-class companies. But knowledge and understanding of strategies are not enough. Let us explain.

Professional athletics are the culmination of the best talent available in the sporting world. Whichever pro sport you look at will typically represent the best players, coaches, and staff in that field. At this level, the players and coaches have proven their ability to perform. Before a game, each coach develops a plan for victory based on the strategies and tactics the coach understands and has seen applied before. On game day, the coach for each side is confident that his or her plan is fundamentally correct. During the pregame show, both strategies look good on the screen.

One team wins and one team loses. Does this mean that the losing coach's plan was incorrect? No, not at the professional level. Which team wins is determined by how well the plan was executed. It is interesting to note that the person who develops the plan is not the one who executes it.

The ability to develop game plans that the team can execute well is a common trait among winning coaches. Winning requires more than just the knowledge of the game's strategy; it takes the understanding of what the team is capable of doing well and what its weaknesses are. Winning requires examination of the competition's capabilities and of the playing conditions. Leaders in manufacturing, like winning coaches, have to develop the plans or programs that *their* companies can execute.

In this chapter we talk about three principles that support the strategies discussed in chapter two:

- Total Quality Management.
- Just-In-Time Manufacturing.
- Administrative Productivity Improvement.

These three tactics are the keys to a game plan for moving a manufacturing company ahead in the competitive 1990s. Each of these programs has been proven to work. The success of a company is dependent on the *execution*, not just the development, of these initiatives. Just as in a sporting match, the team with the most discipline will make fewer mistakes and have to contend with fewer penalties. Penalties and mistakes in manufacturing are the quickest roads to ruin.

Total Quality Management

"Quality" is probably the most misunderstood term in business today.

As with the emotion of love, people are familiar with the concept, yet it is nearly impossible to reach agreement on a definition. This ambiguity seems to make the concept of quality more mysterious and elusive. It leads us to ponder such questions as:

- Is quality an attitude?
- Is high quality more or less expensive?
- Is quality a real or a perceived attribute?
- Who's responsible for quality?

Different people will answer these questions differently. In some aspects quality is an attitude, but attitudes and slogans alone have little appreciable effect on quality output. High quality in terms of overall process efficiency lowers production costs, but high quality in terms of increased product features or aspects raises costs. In some products quality features can be measured, but any measurement not of significance to the customer is irrelevant. In many cases people base purchase decisions on perceived quality. To say that everyone is responsible for quality holds no one accountable, and therefore no one is responsible.

It is quite common for organizations to pursue quality as if it were the Holy Grail. Perhaps the most popular campaign of late is the quest for the Malcolm Baldrige National Quality Award. This award has captured the attention of American management. One client's CEO has offered to pay a full year's salary to all employees of the first division to win the award.

The Baldrige Award is serving a very important role in America. It comes at a time when the country needs something to rally behind. The award is helping to capture the American spirit of competition. It is the epitome of tournament play, complete with the ceremonial presentation of the coveted (and highly marketable) trophy by the president of the United States.

The Baldrige Award criteria and the weight placed on each category are worth discussing. The 1991 examination categories and their relative importance in the judging were as follows:

1. Leadership   9%
2. Information and Analysis   8%
3. Strategic Quality Planning   6%
4. Human Resource Development and Management   15%
5. Management of Process Quality   14%
6. Quality and Operational Results   18%
7. Customer Focus and Satisfaction   30%

These categories indicate that quality is a much broader issue than has been recognized by most domestic manufacturing companies.

In the category of leadership, the examination assesses the demonstrated involvement and direction of the most senior executives in the pursuit of quality excellence. It weighs the communication of quality values both within and outside the company. It also looks at how well the company fulfills its public and societal obligations.

The Baldrige Award recognizes the significance of effective human resource management. The two largest items in the Human Resource Development and Management category are employee involvement and quality education and training. They represent eight of the fifteen points in the field. Involvement equates to the means available to *everyone* in the organization to contribute effectively in achieving the company's quality goals. The education and training portion evaluates how the company decides the requirement and type of training for employees in *all* levels of the organization.

A closer look at the Quality and Operational Results category reveals something interesting: the actual quality of products and services represents only a small fraction of the entire exam. In fact, 92.5 percent of all possible points have nothing to do with the quality of the product! This makes it possible, although not entirely logical, for a company to win the award without having the "best" product. Another interesting point is that the contest for the award is a domestic one. It does not factor in the business reality that we must be competitive in a global market.

The award does, however, place the most weight on customer satisfaction. Twenty percent of the exam's total points are based on the company's knowledge of customer requirements and expectations, determination to satisfy, satisfaction results, and the comparison of those results against competitive offerings. The ability to ascertain the information required in this section, coupled with the examining board's feedback, may arguably be the most valuable aspect of the entire application process.

There is a strong correlation between return on investment, market share, and quality. Superior quality contributes to increased market share. The increase in share shortens the learning curve by increasing experience through volume. Higher quality levels also make a price premium tolerable in the marketplace. The combined effect of these aspects drives increases in profitability. While for the foreseeable future money will continue to be business's life blood, quality will remain a paramount concern.

So, then, what is quality?

Quality is whatever the customer deems it to be in order to satisfy a set of values. These values may be real or perceived, quantifiable or arbitrary. They will vary from market segment to market segment as well as over time. The key determinant for achieving high profit performance is the ability to capture and fulfill the market's current set of quality values.

The Quality Legends

Three men have risen in the field of quality to achieve legendary status: Dr. W. Edwards Deming; Dr. Joseph M. Juran; and Philip Crosby. Deming is credited with educating the Japanese on the application of statistical methods in quality control after the Second World War. His involvement has made such a dramatic impact on that nation that an award in his name was created to recognize outstanding quality performance in Japan. Juran is also given credit for the role he played in the development of quality systems in Japan. Juran was awarded the Second Class of the Order of the Sacred Treasure by the emperor of Japan. It was the highest decoration ever given to a noncitizen of Japan.

Recently we had the rare opportunity to hear Dr. Juran lecture. During the course of his presentation, he used an analogy that dramatized a void in many operations. Dr. Juran compared quality management to financial management in a business: In a well-managed business there is a financial plan. The plan typically spells out an annual projection of sales revenue. The "number" is a compilation of various products and their month-to-month estimated contribution to the plan. From the sales figures, budgets are developed. Each department develops a budget to support the execution of the planned sales. Profitability is estimated by the difference between monthly revenues and monthly expenditures. As the fiscal year progresses, the company's management pays very close attention to actual performance against forecasted estimates. They make changes to expenditures to reflect shortcomings in planned sales. The exercise is continuous and is updated on a monthly basis. It would be disastrous for the company to wait until the close of the year to see if they made plan in aggregate.

The financial model is quite familiar to most managers. The impact of quality and cost is also somewhat familiar to management. But very few companies manage quality with the same discipline with which they manage finance. There is no apparent system to communicate and resolve variations to plans. Monday morning quarterbacking is very much the norm. At the end of the year (or other period), the designated quality people generate summaries on what happened. Nonconformance is an issue, but rarely does it carry the same priority of concern within the organization as financial variances.

It is necessary that management, at all levels, develop a system to plan and then manage actual quality performance to ensure that the plans are met. The mistake that is commonly made is that an objective will be set: for example, 20 percent improvement in end-of-line quality in year X. The objective is only a fantasy if it does not indicate, in detail, where the gains are going to come from and when. Without the specifics laid out, the company is shooting in the dark. It would be like a company hoping to double its sales without identifying where the new business was expected to be found. In the marketing world this exercise is commonly referred to as a "gap analysis."

Long-term quality management needs to develop a gap analysis of its own. It should identify where the company is now (product by product) and where it hopes to be at some future point, in terms related to quality performance. A quality plan will not be worth the paper it's written on if the company lacks the discipline or control systems to execute it.

Elements of a Quality System

Any company that is serious about quality needs a quality system. The system should have a formal structure. It should be treated with the same respect that a company has for its financial and information systems. The support required to develop and maintain such a system is significant. A world-class quality system is capable of yielding world-class results. A system of this importance simply cannot be left as an afterthought to be figured out by the operations staff. It demands the coordinated efforts of the entire organization.

The scope of a good quality system is, therefore, quite large. Any project of this magnitude is doomed from the start without top management commitment. The resources, in terms of time and personnel, to design, develop, and maintain the system will need to be allocated. In most instances the energy required will dwarf the company's existing quality efforts. The benefit will net out when the "after the fact" activities associated with the current system start to go away. The futile drill that the quality and production people run now will prohibit them from developing the "big picture" plan without some relief. Ken McGuire, president of the Manufacturing Excellence Action Coalition, describes the situation as "being too busy drowning to learn how to swim."

Responsibility for determining the company's quality policies rests squarely on senior management. In addition to defining the policy, they must accept accountability for its implementation. The quality policy must be expressed in terms that everyone in the organization can understand and execute. It must be written in a fashion that lends itself to use by all of the people in the company who will ultimately impact its success.

The company must organize itself structurally to support the system. The structure should be designed to define the requisite procedures to be followed. It should clearly designate people's various responsibilities. An important point to remember is that people *can* be held responsible, departments cannot. Without clarity, there can only be confusion.

Since quality is something that goes beyond the physical attributes of a product, the system that governs quality must be broader too. A comprehensive quality system will transcend the various functions of the organization. A world-class program is also desirable in the face of changes occurring in today's business environment.

The most widely accepted set of criteria relating to quality systems is given in the International Organization for Standardization 9000 series. The ISO 9000 standards have been developed in an attempt to harmonize the many national and international requirements in the quality field. The American National Standards Institute and American Society for Quality Control have developed the ANSI/ASQC Q91-94 series, which is consistent with the ISO 9000 series. In accordance with these standards, the elements of a quality system may include:

- Marketing and market research.
- Design/specification engineering and product development.
- Procurement.
- Process planning and development.

- Production.

- Inspection, testing, and examination.

- Packaging and storage.

- Sales and distribution.

- Installation and operation.

- Technical assistance and maintenance.

- Disposal after use.

Take a good look at this list. Compare it to the elements in your company's current quality system. Do you have a formal system that tracks the efforts within each of these functions relative to the clearly stated quality policy? The chances are pretty good that you do not. Yet we venture to guess that your company has a budget for each of these that relates to the overall profit plan.

Our point is that, if we guessed correctly, the financial plan has already captured management's attention, but the quality plan has not. Until management understands the significance of quality and commits to handling quality with the same zeal with which it handles finance, the company quality performance will stagnate at current levels. Just as departments and functions do not set and manage budgets independently of one another, they cannot set quality objectives independently either.

An integral part of the quality system is a quality plan. The plan should include the specific objectives to be met for all existing and any new programs. It needs to identify both responsibility as well as authority during the various phases of execution. The plan defines any procedures or instructions that are used on an ongoing basis. And, finally, the various audit or verification steps and activities should be defined.

The company should look at and evaluate the quality system the way it would any large part of the business. Business is about money. The quality system should be monitored to assess how it is performing in financial terms. The costs associated with the system should incorporate any internal operational costs and any external costs. Some of these external costs may be incurred if outside concerns are required to perform any testing or validation. The internal costs would include all costs related to prevention, appraisal, or failure of the product or process.

Let's take a look at what is involved in some aspects of the various system elements. Perhaps the most logical place to start is marketing. Quality in marketing begins with the assessment of need for a product and the internal capability to deliver it. The definition of an intended market segment and what the value set of that segment is are vital in the product's development or refinement. Quality performance has to do with the accuracy of this information and how clearly marketing can translate the requirements back to the company.

The second element in the system is the specification and design of the product. Many of the tangible aspects of quality are determined in this area. They include the technological interpretation of the customer's needs relative to form, fit, function, and cost. This function impacts the way the product is produced and how quality can be confirmed *during* the process, rather than "inspected in" after the fact.

The amount of purchased content is a large portion of many manufacturers' total cost. Purchased goods and services also have a big impact on total quality. An effective quality procurement program includes clear requirements for all specifications. It has a method of identifying and selecting qualified suppliers. The program has provisions on how quality will be assured and, if need be, verified. It defines how to handle quality disputes between the company and its suppliers. The objective of the program should be to develop a highly responsive and flexible network of relationships to provide high quality with the lowest total cost.

The production function is probably the most commonly thought of area in terms of its ability to impact quality. Based on the number of variables that can be introduced in the production process, and thereby can potentially introduce defects, the thinking may be correct. Quality in production requires controlling the variables, understanding the capabilities of the various processes, and monitoring the progression of products throughout the cycle.

A very powerful and effective way to determine the capability of processes and the impact of variation is through the application of statistics. Dr. W. Edwards Deming is referred to as a statistician by his peers. He was instrumental in developing the practical application of statistical process control (SPC) for manufacturing.

The SPC methods are believed to have led the world's superstars in quality to achievement of parts-per-million defect performance. SPC has broad applicability in both the factory and the office, but it is only one aspect of a comprehensive total quality system.

Just-In-Time

If quality is the most ambiguous term in business, then Just-In-Time (JIT) is the most misinterpreted. Seldom has an acronym sparked as much emotion (both positive and negative) and publicity. The concepts of JIT have been explored by virtually every business and industrial magazine of consequence. Literally libraries of textbooks and video-tapes have been generated on the topic. Thousands of seminars and speeches have been delivered on the subject to hundreds of thousands of people. JIT has become an industry in itself.

It is quite surprising that with all the information available, there is no universally accepted definition of what the term represents. As one might expect, without a common definition, interpretations pro-liferate. Each consulting firm, practitioner organization, academic body, and spectator has its own twist on the basic body of knowledge called JIT.

The underlying theme of Just-In-Time is rather simple: it is the continuous elimination of waste throughout an entire process. Things become more complicated when we begin to translate the theory into practical application.

Despite the simplicity of the concept, most organizations are having problems dealing with it. The problems may actually be a function of the concept's simplicity. A typical problem is that the various factions within many companies cannot agree on what constitutes "waste." Another gray area is deciding where the "process" starts and ends. The larger the organization, the more hotly contested and confused the arguments become.

The Development of Just-In-Time

Henry Ford is credited with actually creating the first "Just-In-Time" factory. The Ford factory could turn iron ore into finished automobiles in thirty-six hours. Not bad for late 1920s and early 1930s technology. This early example of continuous-flow manufacturing was to fade away as mass production turned to batch processing to pursue gains in efficiency.

The JIT saga picks up again in Japan. A crash course in the Japanese socioeconomic situation helps to elucidate why the concept was so well suited to the Japanese. Fundamentally, Japan has very few natural resources and very little space, but one asset readily available to post-war Japan was workers. The achievement of prosperity hinged on the ability to add value to products. This had to be accomplished using maximum efficiency in order to compete globally with superpowers such as the United States.

The Japanese assessed the total conversion cycle for products. All process activities were categorized into two buckets, those that added value and those that added only cost or delay. Any activity that did not raise the inherent value of the product was deemed to be waste.

The Japanese economic situation necessitated the conservative use of available resources. "Waste" was defined to encompass anything more than the absolute minimum use of any resource to process and produce a product, including:

- Scrap.
- Rework.
- Inspection.
- Inventory.
- Overproduction.
- Movement.
- Delay time.

The chronological study of events within the entire cycle revealed that for as much as 90 percent of the time, nothing was happening. Material was literally sitting, waiting for some event to take place. Time was the largest single waste in the chain of production. This initiated the fanatical drive to determine the root cause of any delay or waste in the process. The acceleration of events within the cycle required material to flow "just in time" from one value-adding activity to the next without interruption. The systematic removal of waste led to enormous gains in efficiency, quality, and productivity.

The JIT masters, such as Toyota, developed and refined an entire method to manage manufacturing. The JIT concept involved much more than a coalition of techniques. It represented a new vision of excellence in every aspect of the manufacturing business. The fundamental principles that support JIT transcend the factory and apply to any conversion process or system. But, as in so many other cases, the Japanese were able to adapt a concept and apply it practically. In the case of JIT, they were able to leverage their cultural characteristics of discipline, hard work, and group conformity.

The combination of cultural characteristics and economic need sparked a competitive fire with devastating power. The success of the JIT management system was not instantaneous, however. According to Taiichi Ohno and Shigeo Shingo, who are credited with initiating JIT at Toyota, the process took twenty years to develop and is still being refined. Although the concepts and theory behind JIT are simple, the application is not. To complicate things even further, JIT is a journey, not a destination. You don't ever get there.

The pursuit of manufacturing excellence in America actually seems to be evolving into a sort of religion. It has principles by which its followers abide. They constantly strive to become purer, but recognize they will always be flawed. The JIT following has its zealots and fanatics (who become absorbed by it) along with some less orthodox members. As with religion (unfortunately), people seem to pick and choose which rules they will follow. The JIT religion is complete with written testaments and sacraments, like a pilgrimage to Japan.

Manufacturers that are either disappointed with their current performance, or that have been victimized by the siege, are running to convert. Many seem fascinated by the promise of a JIT operation, which appears almost utopian. Some companies are merely jumping on the bandwagon at the request or pressure of a missionary (such as a large customer, usually deeply involved in JIT). It seems that regardless of where they come from, many of these American manufacturers are fighting desperately to hang on to some old baggage. True to their culture and environment, they yearn for instant gratification.

Let's face it, we Americans are not a patient bunch. Our society wants it *now*. The microwave is quickly making conventional ovens obsolete. The drive-through restaurant is going to be with us forever. We spend millions every year on quick diets and equivalent sums longing for thinner thighs in thirty days. In how many nations can a book called *The One Minute Manager* make it to the bestseller list? Much of the time we tell ourselves that we know better, but that glimmer of hope in the quick fix is too alluring to turn down.

Just-In-Time has captured our attention and affection because it sounds simple. In many sects it is referred to as a back-to-basics program. People have always gravitated to things that promise to help them revisit the "good old days" when things seemed less complicated. JIT has a lot going for it. It has proven itself both in Japan and in a small percentage of U.S. companies. The theories and principles behind the concept cannot mathematically or logically be denied. And emotionally it fills a desire for the return of simpler times. The movement has come at a time when management is vulnerable after years of discouraging results and weary from its search for the silver bullet that will kill the werewolf.

Unlike other programs that have come and gone, Just-In-Time is not another management fad or some smoke-and-mirrors technique. The benefits of JIT are real and measurable. Unfortunately, they do not come easily. You can't go out and buy hardware or software and plug it in. You can't even go out and hire someone to do the job for you. There is no instant pudding.

Consider Just-In-Time a fitness program to get your company in shape. To put things in perspective, survival will depend on making it to the Olympics. A sincere effort will require much more than doing a couple of exercises when your schedule permits. The program will require education on different exercises, diet, and the discipline to follow a regimen that will undoubtedly cause some pain at times. But before you start anything, you need to decide which event you plan on competing in.

Management at the highest level must decide the market segments and positions they want the company to serve. The products and technologies that will be critical to the continued growth of the company must also be determined. The vision cast will determine the program that the company will follow.

A problem common to many companies attempting to JIT their way forward is that the initiatives start without full organizational commitment. As operational managers scramble to try techniques, there is an aura of anticipation. When the techniques work, the march continues. Inevitably, however, the campaign reaches a point where the pain begins. At this threshold, a lack of total commitment will cause the abandonment of the project. The benefits that were achieved may or may not last. If the techniques that were applied run counter to established JIT wisdom, any progress will eventually be lost.

The companies that are genuinely committed do seem to share certain characteristics. First, they understand that world-class performance does not come quickly or easily. Second, they invest in the education of all of their employees, and many, in their suppliers and customers as well. The third, and perhaps most critical, characteristic is discipline. The most successful JIT factories stick to their programs through the tough times with complete management support and fortitude. The JIT masters know that excellence is never achieved, but must be continuously and systematically pursued.

The heart of any Just-In-Time program is continuous improvement. The Japanese term is *Kaizen*. Many JIT initiatives that survive the up-front physical and technical changes die from a stagnation in improvements. A closer look at why these programs stall reveals a common flaw. Continuous improvement must come from everyone in the organization. No company has enough talent to rely solely on their management and technical staff to identify and resolve the seemingly endless amount of waste in a "typical" manufacturing plant.

The determinant of long-term viability is a function of how well all of the company's people understand and contribute to the cause. There needs to be a critical mass of commitment within the organization. Unlike any other program, a JIT initiative must continue to grow or it will start to die. The method used by advanced practitioners to check the pulse of their program is to track the number of suggestions per employee. This measure indicates the direction and rate of improvements. The origin of the suggestions will assist in determining how deeply within the organization the concepts have taken root. The magnitude of the individual ideas are of secondary importance. The primary index is the actual number of received and implemented suggestions. In world-class facilities, it is not uncommon to implement from twelve to over twenty-five ideas per employee per month. Toyota has been the beneficiary of millions of employee ideas over the course of four decades.

Elements of a Just-In-Time System

Like quality, JIT is a concept. Both concepts have principles that govern their application. The principles have almost universal applicability in the management of business. The foundation of Just-In-Time is the elimination of waste within a process. The manner in which the non-value-adding activities are driven out of the cycle can be thought of as a system. Thinking of JIT as a combination of several linked initiatives aids in developing a framework from which to proceed.

Highly efficient manufacturing systems employ the elements listed below in their factories; world-class companies apply these same tactics throughout their business:

- Housekeeping.
- Cellular Manufacturing.
- Fitness for Use.
- Small-Lot Production.
- Quick Changeover.
- Preventive Maintenance.
- Uniform Load Schedules.
- Pull Systems.

Let's take a closer look at how these elements are being used, what they mean, and how they relate to one another as well as to the people.

Housekeeping

The first and most obvious indication of a company's efficiency and quality-consciousness is reflected on the factory floor. A factory that has been neglected is quite easy to spot. It is typically filthy. The condition of most factories we have visited should be an embarrassment to management. What makes the situation even more pronounced is the sharp dichotomy between the work environments in the office and those of the shop.

Is it any wonder that there is friction between the folks who are working in the dungeon and those who work in the castle? Is it any wonder that there is a striking resemblance to medieval class systems that undermines cooperation? Is it a surprise that managers and technical support people spend an absolute minimum amount of time in the dungeon? Why is it so bewildering that many bright young people stay out of the manufacturing careers that involve working in the shop? How can people be shocked that quality and productivity are awful in plants where it is impossible to make any sense amid the clutter and chaos?

In physics there is a law that might hold the secret: the law governs the quantity called entropy. Entropy is a measure of the degree of disorder of a system, and the law says that things move from a state of order to a more disordered state unless energy is applied to the system. Astronomers use this law to explain the expansion of the universe after the "Big Bang." We use it to explain what happens to our desks after a while if we don't keep cleaning up. The same law seems to hold true for the garage, the yard, and other, more personal aspects of our lives. Without the constant input of organized energy these things dissipate.

The same principle holds true for business, in spades. Consider how many projects and initiatives your organization has started over the years. How many well-founded and practical projects just seemed to fade away? Unless they received constant energy (attention, time, money), they evaporated. If we look at the factory, what has happened is obvious. Factories do not start out dirty and chaotic. They gradually get worse as priorities change. Without the constant influx of money, attention, and other resources, they erode into the state in which we now find them.

To turn around these effects, we need literally to clean up our act. The benefits of a well-kept facility go beyond the obvious aesthetic improvement. It provides the affirmation to the company's employees, customers, suppliers, and competitors that the energy is back. An effective housekeeping program hammers a stake in the ground that signifies that the change has begun. In relative terms, it is an easy way to commence what will be a long and continuously more trying campaign to become a world-class competitor. Also, it will indicate the level of discipline that the organization has to plan, develop, install, and then maintain the program. The crucial indicator is the ability to maintain the initiative.

There are five aspects common to the best housekeeping practices as demonstrated by companies throughout the world recognized for both quality and productivity:

- Arrangement.
- Orderliness.
- Cleanliness.
- Constancy.
- Discipline.

The first of these, arrangement, is simply having a place for everything and then keeping everything where it belongs. Many shops are cluttered due to the accumulation of odds and ends over the years. The first step is physically to take everything out of an area and only replace those items absolutely necessary for production. Everything that is put back should have a permanent home. The analogy we like to use is the workshop pegboard. The pegboard has an outline that silhouettes each tool. Each tool has one spot on the board. Those of you who have such a pegboard in your home know how much easier it makes doing a project. The rest of us dread having to do even the most basic repair because we know the biggest pain will be rummaging around the house to find the tools.

Having a fixed location for everything in the factory saves time otherwise lost looking for equipment, tools, fixtures, or maybe even materials.

A second advantage is that you know immediately that something is missing when you go to its fixed location and find it gone. By removing the piles of unnecessary junk around work areas, space will be recovered to use more productively. In many cases, not having the stuff lying around will also make the workplace safer.

The second aspect is orderliness, which involves making some rules about how much of what goes where. In the pegboard analogy, only one hammer fits on the peg. The silhouette makes the shape and size of the hammer that belongs on that hook obvious. Even people who can't tell the difference between a ball peen and a claw can see where it belongs if they are holding it. It provides a way to simplify and make obvious what is right and wrong.

Companies are applying the same concept in several ways. One example is footprinting where equipment goes. The number of footprints indicate visually (the sense people use 80 percent of the time to learn) how many pieces go there. A second example is mapping out how material flows from one operation to the next or when to replenish material. Orderliness allows the quick and clear identification of a problem because it stands out. In the current plant environment one has a hard time figuring out what is supposed to be anywhere.

Cleanliness is the first thing that comes to people's minds when they hear "housekeeping." Without a doubt, plain cleanliness is a requirement for high quality. People would rather work in a clean place than in a filthy one. A clean shop means one less issue to pull operator morale down. Clean factories also seem to instill a greater sense of pride among all employees. And people tend to keep a clean place clean. For example, people are much more likely to throw candy wrappers and assorted other trash onto the floor of a movie theater than the floor of a hospital. In a cluttered factory, no one even notices the accumulation of "new" junk. But in some of the highest-quality organizations, you would be hard-pressed to find a cigarette butt on the floor. In fact, some Japanese manufacturing companies require you to remove your street shoes and put on slippers to tour their plant!

It is important to note that a normally spotless factory has benefits beyond better morale. To keep a facility clean requires maintenance. It becomes rather obvious that a normally spotless machine that starts to trickle oil down its frame has a problem that needs attention. But if the "normal" condition of the machine is to be grimy and surrounded by a four-inch dune of sand-like material, who is even going to notice another trickle?

The object of constancy, the fourth aspect, is to develop a routine. The routine will grow into habit, which then becomes second nature to people. It is very much like brushing your teeth in the morning. It is something you do almost without thinking. And, if you do forget, you feel very conscious of having forgotten. The habit in the factory helps to ensure that things are put in their appropriate place as a matter of course. The additional benefit is that routines help to point out opportunities for improvement. For example, if you had to go down the hall to the linen closet to get the toothpaste twice a day before you brushed your teeth, it would not take long for you to recognize that there must be a better location for the toothpaste. The routine that operators will follow to retrieve supplies needed to perform their duties will identify the best places to keep what they need. The same principle holds true for any process or activity in the company. Improvements are easily recognized when a series of events is performed over and over using the same method. But, if an activity sequence is performed differently each time it is done, it becomes much more difficult to spot areas for improvements in the pattern.

The fifth aspect of housekeeping is discipline. Cleaning the factory from stem to stern and arranging everything in an orderly fashion will yield short-lived benefits if the organization lacks discipline. Speaking from experience, a pegboard in the home workshop can quickly become worthless at the hands of children who naturally lack the discipline to follow the program. If there is no penalty for noncompliance to agreed terms, then there is no hope of continued benefit. Discipline is one form of energy required to fight off the entropy that is certain to undermine the housekeeping effort. People can learn discipline.

We do not wish to enter a psychological opinion on how to create discipline. Whether reward and punishment are effective is an object of debate. We would simply like to point out that the organizational and societal cultures that exhibit high levels of personal discipline excel in competitive performance. At the risk of being too general, American manufacturing has not traditionally demonstrated well-disciplined performance. Whether this is a cultural or a societal quirk is irrelevant. The critical point is that this trait handicaps our ability to compete in global markets. It is also one that can be, and in several instances is currently being, overcome.

Cellular Manufacturing

In a traditional, functionally organized factory, equipment and operations are physically arranged by type. All of the milling machines in one department, the lathes in another, the grinders in a third, and so on ad infinitum. These functional departments were developed to max-imize the efficiency of that particular function. Unfortunately, this type of organization is virtually impossible to balance in terms of capacity or output. Each group has its own lead times and capacities that are subject to daily variations. The problem of balance is further exacer-bated by the physical dislocation of sequential departments. The larger the facility, the more difficult it is to coordinate tasks and to manage effectively.

A cellular manufacturing environment physically or logically links the sequential operations required to produce a complete product or family of parts. The objective of a manufacturing cell is to eliminate any non-value-adding activities to process a product. It utilizes minimal space and material handling, and simplifies the flow of product through multiple operations to accelerate the total end-to-end cycle time. It also facilitates job rotation of employees. A manufacturing cell seeks to maximize the output of the cell, not to maximize the utilization or efficiency of any one piece of equipment within the cell.

A tremendous advantage of cells is that they are simpler both to manage and to understand. Cells are more "user-friendly" than func-tionally organized factories. They simplify, clarify, and focus the work that needs to be done to meet specific objectives relative to time, qual-ity, and cost. Manufacturing cells avoid what may be the greatest ob-stacle in manufacturing, the inability to get your arms around the complete system. Cells also virtually eliminate contention for resources, which invariably costs time.

Fitness for Use

The fitness-for-use concept means that at each step of the process the supplier delivers to the next operation a product or service that is fit to be used without further delay or activity. Delivery of a quality prod-uct, precisely when needed, requires intimate knowledge of how the product will be used by the next operation. Fitness for use is most effective when the elements of housekeeping are in place and products flow within a cell. The concept raises awareness of how each person or operation contributes to the overall performance of the plant. It encourages the assumption of ownership and responsibility for con-tinuous improvement of the process.

Small-Lot Production

As already mentioned, the largest single category of waste in the manufacturing cycle is time. In what are considered to be the most efficient factories in the world, the work-to-wait ratio (value/nonvalue) is 50/ 50. The most common range of figures we have seen in companies not part of the upper echelon is more like 3–25 percent work to 75–97 percent wait. Companies must drive to eliminate the root causes of delays in the process.

A primary cause of delay, or waiting, is attributable to batch sizes. The larger the bucket or queue of work, the longer each individual piece must wait in line for its turn. In most traditional plants, these processing batches are run completely through one operation and then moved on to the subsequent operation. Step by step, batch by batch, it becomes painfully obvious that most of an individual part's life is spent waiting in line.

What many American managers have done to attempt to accelerate the cycle is to purchase faster machines. Unfortunately, the actual time consumed by the "work," or the machine, is tiny. Even if the new technology reduced the time it takes to process each piece, it would do little to the total time it takes to run through the entire batch. The new equipment may in fact make matters worse. First of all, the equipment was justified on the basis of its speed, so the company naturally will want to run more parts through it. Second, the introduction of the "supermachine" will throw the synchronization of individual steps in the complete process out of balance, with the net result of little to no improvement in the total cycle.

Reducing the size of the batch will shorten the amount of time any individual piece sits waiting to get on a machine or to get worked on. In the ideal situation, a batch size of one, each unit would flow uninterrupted from one operation to another through the process. Eliminating the possibility of waiting would result in a dramatically improved rate and, therefore, efficiency. In this scenario, the only remaining non-value-adding steps left are those required to move the part from one operation to the next. The added benefit of small-lot production is that it will highlight the opportunity to connect operations in cells.

Small lot sizes increase flexibility. Since the time in queue before any operation shrinks, the opportunity to start the next different job comes sooner. This improves the ability to react to changes in requirements coming from any direction. The response time to change is directly proportional to the size of process and transfer batches within the cycle.

Quick Changeover

In many of today's factories we simply are not prepared to start manufacturing in small batches. Small batches would mean that every time we ran a job, we would be running quantities sufficient for shorter periods. That means an increase in the frequency with which each part would need to be run. Based on how long it now typically takes to change over machines, lines, or test stands, this simply would not be possible. The manufacturers that have become serious about waste elimination have focused on reducing the time required to set up equipment. The benefit of reducing setup times is that it makes small-lot production feasible.

Running more parts than are actually needed consumes machine capacity prematurely. The benefits of increased machine capacity realized by running smaller lots far outweigh the incremental benefit of reduced labor content associated with the actual setup. By reducing the penalty (real or perceived) of changing processes over, flexibility is improved. The companies that continue to tolerate long setup and changeover times are caught in a trap. They will feel compelled to run larger batches in order to decrease the frequency of changeovers. Large batches waste the limited resources of time and money.

Preventive Maintenance

Once a plant starts to run smaller lots, the amount of time buffered by inventory is shaved down. Leaner inventory levels demand that equipment be ready to perform when needed. Upsets or equipment downtime, which occur unexpectedly, will shut off downstream operations. Random failures are much too costly for us not to try to avoid them.

The best analogy that comes to mind is the airline industry. The cost of equipment failure for an airplane in flight is far too high for anyone just to wait until something breaks before it gets attention. The airlines follow strict maintenance and inspection programs. Despite the rigor of such a program, accidents still happen. Fortunately, preventable mechanical failures have very rarely been the cause of a catastrophe.

The leaner and tighter a plant wants to run, the more important it is to approach a total maintenance program with the recognition and management support that it deserves. Shutting lines down due to sporadic part supply as a result of chronic or intermittent machine problems was a common element of early JIT programs. Failure to structure an effective program can actually undermine a company's JIT initiative.

Uniform Load Schedule

There are several aspects of a traditional, functional factory that inhibit its ability to operate smoothly. One of the most pronounced deficiencies is a lack of balance, which, within the various functions and operations, results in bottlenecks that throttle output. Balance is a key ingredient and common element of successful JIT operations.

One way to gauge or initiate the balance of a plant is through its schedule. The schedule permits the calculation of necessary production rates in specific units of time. The most advanced JIT manufacturers are paced by what is occasionally referred to as a drumbeat. These plants break their processes into elements that fall into synchronization with the drumbeat. A facility whose production processes are organized in cells with very little inventory is simpler to manage and balance. Lack of focus in a traditional factory prohibits balancing by its management.

Balanced production processes normalize the draw on the plant's resources. The key task is to break any seemingly large problem into a series of small elements that are much simpler to manage and predict. Production resources can then be assessed to fulfill each individual element or event against a known rate. The genuinely world-class factories quite literally run like clockwork.

Pull Systems

It is pretty common knowledge that the trend in manufacturing has been to reduce inventory. Plants are making great strides in managing the levels of inventory they need to run the shop. Many appear to hit a wall once they reach a certain level. When they get to this point they seem to have bottomed out. The way that they proceed to squeeze out inefficiencies further is by using a pull system. It is important to note that the true JIT masters went to pull systems only after the other aspects we've discussed were in place.

Pull systems move material and work through the manufacturing cycle from the end of a process to the beginning. The underlying principle of a pull system is to draw necessary items only in quantities needed, just as they are needed. A pull system can work well if the supply source is in a state of readiness when it receives the signal to produce a requirement and has the capacity to fill the request completely. Obviously, if the demand on any source is continuously variable in quantity and sporadic in frequency, the system will need to be buffered to prevent downtime in the loop. The effects of demand variability are cumulative and tend to magnify both peaks and lulls. This is why it is important to smooth the demand drivers within the cycle through load balancing and capacity buffering.

Capacity buffering is a means to provide reactive capabilities when natural disruptions occur. The most common method used to buffer capacity is to limit the volume on any operation or process. By setting a maximum usage cap of, say, 70 percent normal, you have actually given yourself the capability to handle a 30 percent surge. What many managers have done in the past is schedule discrete operations at 100 percent and then buffer demand fluctuations with surplus inventory. The deliberate underutilization of assets is a very effective way to build flexibility into the system. The cost penalty associated with inflexibility will be very painful moving forward. The interesting point is that excess and obsolete inventory is frequently written off, while excess reactive capacity never is. The scheduling of any discrete operation at 100 percent is an artificial and archaic way to get higher productivity. It assures that process imbalances result in inventory and lost efficiency.

One advantage of pull systems is that they reflect the actual consumption rate and guard against the usage of assets earlier than is necessary. The systems employ signaling methods that can be containers, cards (*Kanbans*), or, in more advanced applications, electronic signals. In general, the systems that are controlled visually are the most user-friendly and most easily tuned. The systems act as the communication link among independent processes. Previous systems tended to produce supplies to a fixed schedule regardless of actual demand changes in downstream processes. To make this situation even worse, there was poor, if any, feedback in between logically and physically disassociated departments. It does not take a genius to figure out that pull systems make much more sense than the traditional scheduling systems, if for no other reason than because they promote better communications within the plant.

Used effectively, pull systems can help manufacturers crash through the floor they hit as they suck inventory out of their operations. They can generate vastly improved inventory turns, which frees up capital. The danger, however, is that the systems are only minimally effective if process quality is not in control or the other aspects of JIT are not in place.

Administrative Productivity

JIT principles are often thought of as factory concepts. But if you embrace JIT as the process to eliminate waste, then wherever there is waste there is an opportunity to apply the JIT concepts. For years, companies have concentrated on waste in the factory. Take a look at the office. There is enormous opportunity to reduce waste and improve productivity within the administrative functions of most companies.

An interesting pattern has evolved over the last three decades. If we break down (into categories of overhead, materials, and labor) the average cost distribution trends for the manufacturing industry and track them since the 1960s, the following outcomes become apparent:

- Direct labor content has decreased by approximately 40 percent.

- Overhead has doubled and is the largest cost of doing business for most companies.

- The number of nonproduction workers (managers, supervisors, support personnel, etc.) has increased almost five times as fast as the direct labor workforce.

Reducing Overhead

After digesting these data, take a step back and ask why we are continuing to focus the vast majority of our efforts on reducing the cost of direct labor? A couple of reasons come to mind. First, this is the way we've always thought about it. Second, direct labor is politically the least powerful and by far the easiest to victimize. Although this may have been an effective strategy when direct labor represented a significant portion of the cost, it is now financially less beneficial and useful only to primitively managed companies and sweatshops. It is clearly the wrong approach for the majority of manufacturing companies that have an understanding of contemporary manufacturing economics. These organizations should focus on reducing overhead.

Although there is no panacea, administrative productivity improvement programs can significantly reduce overhead in the following ways:

- By creating self-sufficiency in the workforce through a concerted effort to leverage quasi-management and support responsibilities.
- By improving the efficiency of the administrative process flows that support the manufacturing function.

Specifically, an administrative productivity improvement program is defined as a systematic process to eliminate the cost-adding activities of any process flow. The focus of any well-designed administrative productivity improvement program should be on improving the overall value-adding to cost-adding ratio for those functions not on the factory floor. In a sense, it can be considered white-collar Just-In-Time.

Traditionally, companies have attempted to improve administrative productivity through one of the following three approaches: across-the-board budget reductions; freezing expenditures on equipment, supplies, or hiring; or massive personnel displacements. Generally, these approaches have failed to achieve any long-term meaningful improvements. Common reasons for failure have ranged from selling the initiative as a time-bounded project (when the project is over, they staff up again and go back to the old inefficient processes), to insufficient employee involvement and commitment.

A structured and logical approach begins with the application of a number of data-collection tools and techniques to analyze process flows and organizational subsystems. Typically, the initial project focus is on studying work flows, work methods, and reporting relationships/ job design to identify improvement opportunities. Organizational subsystems such as the culture/climate characteristics, information system capabilities, and Human Resource policies/programs are also analyzed to determine how they impact administrative productivity.

During the second stage, improvement opportunities are studied and prioritized. These opportunities usually focus on eliminating cost-adding activities, redesigning office layouts to facilitate access to needed resources (such as people, equipment, and reference materials), and redesigning jobs to leverage work to the lowest level (this can include self-directed work teams). After management has approved these opportunities, detailed work plans are created to guide the implementation efforts.

A well-designed and well-managed program will be self-funding and can yield tangible results in as little as three months. The more successful programs tend to utilize an interdisciplinary approach drawing heavily from such functional areas as Change Management, Industrial Engineering, Ergonomics, Organization Development, Human Resource Development, and Job Design.

Companies that have successfully implemented an administrative productivity program report the following positive operational and quality of worklife benefits (benefits will vary depending on the structure and focus of the program):

- Improved customer service/satisfaction.

- Streamlined throughput times.

- Improved variance identification and analysis.

- Improved in-process quality.

- Simplified operations.

- Increased spans of control.

- Improved performance measurement and feedback.

- Reduced document transactions.

- Improved utilization of office space and equipment.

- Development of a self-sustaining work methods improvement process.

- Reduced number of delays and bottlenecks.

Institutionalizing Change

The area that provides organizations with the greatest amount of trouble is institutionalizing the improvements and keeping the old ways from creeping back. There are four courses of action that should be undertaken to institutionalize change: periodically evaluate the program; balance workloads; modify reporting relationships; and modify appropriate Human Resource policies.

As mentioned earlier, an outgrowth of the administrative productivity improvement process is a self-sufficient operating workforce. Since this empowered workforce has taken on some supervisory/management and technical support responsibilities, supervisory/management spans of control should be expanded. The traditional roles of supervisors and managers should change from directing employees to coaching, facilitating, and training employees.

Any support freed up should be redirected toward completing higher-level activities. Staffing reductions that result from this transition should be handled with extreme caution. A program that starts to be associated with a body count may be undermined by those responsible for its initial success. We strongly recommend that, if at all possible, excess personnel be transferred, given some optional incentives, or removed through natural attrition.

The last step in closing the loop is to modify the appropriate Human Resource policies to support the changes. In most instances this will include the following: revising performance standards; the performance management system for the operating workforce, supervisors, and managers; the employee selection policy/criteria; the orientation policy for new hires; and the promotion policy.

A company's reward system must also be closely scrutinized to assess whether it is rewarding the desired behaviors and output measures. Since most individuals' behavior tends to be self-satisfying, it is of integral importance to ensure that the reward system closely rewards compliance and punishes noncompliance to any new changes.

In conclusion, the three tactical principles we have presented in this chapter embody the frame of how world-class companies are organizing themselves to stay ahead in today's competitive environment. We are now going to take a more in-depth look at the support systems needed to implement and sustain these initiatives over the long haul. From education to compensation and measurement, we hope to share our observations on the critical aspects that many internally driven initiatives discount. We believe that the executional details surrounding the "people" side of change are far more important to the viability of truly continuous improvement than are the technical aspects. It is also the most difficult area to impact, due to the historical border conflicts and political superstructure in place in most companies. The criticality of these people issues warrants our devotion to it of a major portion of this book: proper execution will spell the difference between success and failure.

Chapter **4**

The Importance of Communication and Education

The first three chapters of this book discussed the characteristics of future competition, strategies for survival, and the importance of improving productivity. True success in implementing organizational change is dependent upon two factors: (1) identifying the correct strategies, tactics, and initiatives to implement; and (2) being able to execute them successfully. In this and the next two chapters, we will discuss the key success factors for achieving world-class performance.

Over the last several years we have collectively worked with many organizations to assist them in implementing change. We have also conducted extensive research on the subject of organizational change. Recently we completed a survey of presidents, senior executives, and top managers in Fortune 500 companies, asking them about their experiences in implementing change. The participants were asked to provide feedback on a recent initiative that they had implemented. The questions included:

- What internal or external conditions precipitated the change?
- What approach was used to plan and implement the change?
- What were the major obstacles encountered during the planning and implementation process?
- How were the obstacles overcome?
- What methods were used to assess and bring about needed change in your organization's culture?

When one studies the approach used by the organizations that have the best "track record" in implementing change, five common themes soon become apparent. These common themes are the key success factors that *must* be addressed for an organization to implement change effectively. They are:

- The utilization of a focused communication strategy.
- Timely and targeted education.
- Total systems integration.
- Employee involvement.
- A structured and focused approach to implementing change.

Since communications and education overlap so much—you can't do one without the other—we focus our discussion in this chapter on these first two key success factors together. Employee involvement is addressed in Chapter 5, the concept of total systems integration is discussed in Chapter 6, and Chapter 7 presents a structured approach or methodology for operationalizing the concepts.

The Importance of a Communication Strategy

A large organization is analogous to a battleship. When one turns a battleship to avoid uncertain conditions, a specific course must be plotted and communicated to the crew.

In the business world there are many unanticipated market conditions that necessitate quick reaction. Organizations that are most successful tend to utilize a communication strategy to alert stakeholders (anyone who impacts or is impacted by the organization—including the community, suppliers, customers, employees, and the like) both inside and outside the organization of potential problems or to clarify changes in strategic direction. We believe an effective communication strategy consists of the following components:

- A clearly articulated vision.

- Redundant or overlapping mechanisms (one-on-one discussions, meetings, press releases, internal publications, videotapes, social events, etc.) to communicate this vision to all impacted stakeholders.

- Channels to solicit stakeholder concerns/input (the most successful communication strategies use vehicles that facilitate top–down, bottom–up, and horizontal communications).

Vision

The first and most important place to begin is with a vision. Like many other frequently used business terms (such as quality or productivity), "vision" means different things to different people. We believe from our consulting practice that a well-developed vision achieves three objectives: (1) it communicates the desired future state of the organization in a manner that is believable and that will foster stakeholder commitment; (2) it describes the beliefs and attitudes valued by management; and (3) it clarifies the business thrust or focus of effort. Without a sound vision, stakeholders lack the direction and motivation to "bite the bullet" and embrace, rather than resist, change.

A Fortune 500 manufacturing company with which we have worked has developed an excellent example of a well-written vision statement. Their vision is comprised of the following five components:

1. We are an organization that is totally customer driven. Interactions with customers are an accepted and encouraged business practice;
2. We are an organization that facilitates effective and special communications where business objectives, strategies, and results are known to all;
3. We are an organization that is managed by the employees. Problems are handled by those closest to the facts;

4. We are an organization that is people driven and where compensation and rewards are equitably distributed based on performance;

5. We are an organization with a culture that fosters continuous improvement where innovation is encouraged, mistakes tolerated, and the only truly wrong action is inaction.

If you are one of the "lucky ones" who have been charged with the development of a vision during your career, you know the process is demanding, iterative, and at times frustrating. It is difficult to create a statement behind which all stakeholders can rally. And like the change management process itself, there are a host of different ways to communicate the vision. Some organizations use a top–down approach, with senior management creating the vision with little or no input from employees. Other organizations have taken great pains to include key stakeholder groups in the vision formulation. Some managers perceive the different approaches as a trade-off between time and cost versus the level of stakeholder commitment desired. The more successful companies soon find it is not a trade-off: if you don't have employee commitment and understanding, then you really don't have a worthwhile vision! To ensure commitment, we recommend a closed-loop process. This usually starts with senior management developing a first draft of a vision. Since this group is commonly charged with acting on data from a variety of stakeholders (e.g., customers, employees, competitors) and sources (market research, internal strengths/weaknesses audit, operational performance data, etc.). This draft is then disseminated to appropriate stakeholders and revised until all key parties support the vision.

Once the vision has been developed, the challenge becomes communicating the vision to the stakeholders. This represents an untapped opportunity for most organizations. The higher a manager's position in an organization, the more communications reaching him or her tend to be filtered. This distortion of information can have tremendous impacts on organizational effectiveness. An excellent example of this is something that commonly occurred during the Vietnam War. If a squad (approximately twelve men) engaged the enemy in a firefight, the first lieutenant would report back to the firebase the number of enemy casualties (ten men). When this was reported to divisional headquarters, the count rose to 100. By the time it reached the Pentagon, it was

1,000. It appeared we had an army full of Rambos and Dirty Harrys. The major risk of filtered communications is poor decision quality because decisions are based on erroneous information. This type of filtering occurs when information is communicated in only one direction.

The President and Chief Operating Officer of a Fortune 100 company echoes our sentiments regarding the difficulty of communicating a vision:

> If there is one thing I have learned on the subject of communicating our vision, it is the need to repeat, repeat, and repeat the specifics of the strategic message. The broad-brush approach just doesn't work.

Another executive of a multinational Fortune 500 company shares a similar perception:

> A recent article in a business journal quoted a number of CEOs who said that you cannot repeat and reinforce your strategy enough. They felt—and so do I—that you cannot assume your employees will retain the strategic message. We have an annual planning meeting to review our strategy to a fare-thee-well. At quarterly reviews and meetings with employees, our officers continually talk about basic beliefs and our vision. We never assume that everyone knows it all. We continuously reinforce it.

A growing number of organizations have closely followed the principles of communication we have outlined. Their reward has been significant operational improvements that have catapulted them into the limelight. Their stories are deceptively simple. Instead of making huge investments in robots and automation, they invested their resources in improving organizational communications and educating their stakeholders. Here are a few of these success stories.

Success Stories

Blount Inc., formerly a part of Omark Industries (Omark is widely recognized for its success in implementing JIT), is the world's largest manufacturer of cutting chain, guide bars, and drive sprockets for chain saws. It employs over 2,000 people, has annual sales in excess of $160 million, and does business in over 120 countries. Headquartered in

Montgomery, Alabama, it is organized into three business segments: manufacturing, construction, and resource recovery.

In 1982 the Oregon Cutting Systems (OCS) Division of Blount Inc. embarked on a strategy focused on continuous quality improvement. Their program was based on the following five rules: (1) streamline the organizational structure to minimize the number of organizational levels; (2) cross-train employees so that they are able to perform a variety of jobs; (3) modify the culture to foster information availability at all levels; (4) reduce the bureaucracy (administrative policies, work rules, etc.); and (5) change the prevalent management style from a reactive to a proactive focus.

Oregon Cutting Systems attributes a large part of the success of its continuous quality improvement initiative to the emphasis it places on organizational communications and education. A communication strategy was developed that focused on creating a vision, communicating it to employees, and developing conflict-management mechanisms to address employee concerns. All employees also participated in training sessions on such topics as process improvement, problem prevention, quality concepts, statistical process control, and customer service measurement.

An effective initiative not only makes people feel better about working by improving morale and motivation, but it also provides significant operational and strategic benefits. Listed below are some of OCS's key quality-of-worklife (QWL) and operational accomplishments from 1982 to 1989:

- Management levels were decreased from seven to four.

- Five plants were consolidated into three.

- Throughput decreased by 70 percent at their Portland plant.

- Absenteeism was reduced from 5 percent to 3 percent.

Milliken is another company that has found itself in the limelight recently because of their commitment to manufacturing excellence. This privately held company, founded over 120 years ago, places a heavy emphasis on education as a tactic for making change happen. Headquartered in Spartanburg, South Carolina, the company employs over 14,000 people in 28 businesses generating annual sales in excess of $1 billion. It manufactures over 48,000 different textile and chemical products ranging from apparel and automotive fabrics to specialty chemicals and floor coverings for more than 8,000 customers worldwide.

Milliken has distinguished itself as a world-class company in the quality arena. It has won a number of quality awards, including the 1989 Malcolm Baldrige Award, and several of its European plants have qualified for the 9001 Quality Award. Milliken utilizes a strategy that focuses on the following four areas:

- Maximize customer satisfaction: They are the industry leaders in quality and on-time delivery.

- Create an egalitarian culture: There are no time clocks, no private offices, no reserved parking, no status rankings—subordinates, hourly, exempt. All employees are called Associates.

- Develop a strong people focus: Through their centralized training function, called Milliken University, the organization contracts with a number of outside consultants and noted academics to provide education on a wide range of topics. Each Production Associate receives at least twenty hours of classroom education per year, and managers participate in approximately forty hours of education per year. The education provided covers topics ranging from manufacturing strategy to housekeeping and teamwork. In addition to formal classroom training, Milliken also emphasizes cross-training and employs self-directed work teams and skill-based pay in a number of locations.

- Facilitate vertical and horizontal communications: Milliken is deeply invested in a program they call "Pursuit of Excellence." This process improvement program relies heavily on eliminating barriers to internal and external communications. An integral part of this program is survey feedback. Management regularly surveys customers and employees to determine their current perceptions regarding a number of variables such as customer satisfaction and product quality. The organization also uses a number of other vehicles, including their recognition program, which relies heavily on nonfinancial awards such as personal letters and handshakes. They also have pioneered the use of Customer Partnership Teams to enhance communications with suppliers. These teams provide real-time communications between Milliken and its suppliers to cut across organizational boundaries and solve problems quickly.

Globe Metallurgical, Inc., is another company synonymous with quality excellence. In the last six years it has won the following quality awards: the Malcolm Baldrige Award (in the small business category); the first Shigeo Shingo Award presented to an American company for manufacturing excellence; Ford's Q1 and Q101 Awards; General Motors' Mark of Excellence Award; and the United States Senate Productivity Award. Globe has also purchased a company in England called Materials and Methods that was certified in British Standard 5057 and in ISO 9002.

Globe Metallurgical, Inc., is part of the ferroalloy industry, which has been in a precipitous decline since the 1970s. During this period the industry has been hit hard by large increases in electricity and coal prices, tightening environmental regulations, and high labor rates.

Globe Metallurgical began its journey to world-class performance in the mid-1980s. Many of their customers (foundries, steel companies, and metallurgical businesses) began demanding improved quality, increased operational flexibility, and shorter lead times. As is the case in most successful initiatives, the transition followed a top–down approach, beginning with senior management, who initially focused on educating themselves on the latest quality, customer service, and productivity improvement concepts. Once the senior group had a conceptual understanding of these concepts, they began networking with and visiting leading companies to learn more about change management.

The cornerstone of Globe's success is its Quality, Efficiency, and Cost (QEC) program. This program is guided by a management steering committee that oversees the program. One of their most important undertakings was to develop and communicate a vision to all employees. Condensed and simply stated, their vision was to be the highest-quality and lowest-cost producer in their industry.

Once the vision was communicated to and accepted by employees, a comprehensive training program was designed that addressed a number of tactical and strategic issues relating to employee empowerment, quality improvement, and customer service improvement. Most of their plants were then reorganized around teams (either department, crossfuntional, project, or interplant). With a vision for a blueprint describing the desired end-state, employees were charged with applying the education and making positive change happen.

Like each of the other companies discussed, management at Globe Metallurgical attributes a good portion of their success to the effectiveness of their education and communications initiatives. Once their employees knew and accepted the vision, they created a culture that facilitated innovation and positive change. Arden Sim, CEO of Globe Metallurgical, credits the quality improvements with significantly reducing costs and allowing the company to operate at 90% of capacity while the industry as a whole is operating at 40%. He estimates that for every dollar the company has invested in quality it has realized a return of 4 dollars.

Timely and Targeted Education

Until recently, most organizations thought of training and education as interchangeable terms. Training was something done for the "people" who worked in the dirty, disorganized environment called the shop floor. Training was needed to get the people to respond more quickly to the various bells and whistles that told them when to eat lunch or take a break. Education was something provided to professionals as a perk. (Since we didn't really pay for performance, we couldn't give them good raises; the next best thing was a couple of days out of the office in a nice city participating in a seminar.) In either case, training and education were viewed as afterthoughts when implementing an initiative. Only when there was considerable employee resistance would education and training be considered as a reactive intervention to re-energize a stalled initiative.

The meanings of these two terms, however, are quite different, and timely and targeted education is critical to the success of most world-class manufacturing initiatives. First, let's differentiate the terms. You train dogs or cats or animals in the circus to perform tricks. You do not train people. Education is a process, not a program. The process begins with the development of a curriculum. Simply said, what are the competencies (e.g., skills, knowledge, and experiences) that impacted stakeholders need to develop to assimilate an initiative? Once the competencies that are needed in the *future* have been identified for each group, the *existing* competency levels may be assessed. Education, either on-the-job or in the classroom, should then be designed and presented in the appropriate sequence to close competency deficiencies. Since we have designed and delivered many seminars, we can offer the following guidelines for designing timely and targeted education:

1. Start the education process with the seniormost managers who are impacted by the initiative. In most instances this initial education should focus on a conceptual understanding of and the strategic rationale behind world-class manufacturing.

2. Make sure there is an appropriate balance between education that addresses the technical and the nontechnical sides of the initiative. Our collective experience suggests that it is significantly easier to sell management on providing funding for technical education (e.g., fitness for use, SPC) than it is to get resources for softer areas (e.g., team building, conflict management). Most organizations that already have education programs in place tend to focus inordinately on technical subject areas. This is not terribly startling because many of the trainers are line and staff managers whose strengths tend to be in the technical areas (e.g., operations, information systems, engineering). More often than not, this orientation lends itself to a technical, numbers-driven style of management. Education in the soft areas is not highly valued and is looked upon as some sort of "charm school."

3. As the education progresses down the hierarchy, it is important to provide tactical, or "how-to," education to the troops who are responsible for implementing the initiative.

Tektronix, Inc., is an excellent example of an organization that places a strong emphasis on education as a means to support an overall change effort. Founded in 1946 by Howard Vollum, Jack Murdock, and three associates in the back of a Portland, Oregon, radio shack, Tektronix, Inc., is organized around three business groups: Test and Measurement, Communications, and Visual Systems. In less than 50 years, it has grown to over 15,000 employees worldwide and has a number of plants in the United States, Europe, the Orient, and South America.

In 1987 the Technologies Division embarked on a strategy that shifted from a historical focus on improving the manufacturing operations to focusing on improving the *overall* business cycle. In order to achieve this strategy, management embarked on three initiatives: JIT, TQC, and MRPII. One of the first actions that management focused on was developing a detailed curriculum of education for each affected stakeholder group. This education addressed the following topics:

- The strategic benefits of each initiative.

- A conceptual overview of JIT, TQC, and MRPII.

- How to become a Class A MRP company.

Once the education was assimilated, management reorganized employees around work teams composed of Manufacturing, Purchasing, Engineering, and other support functions. These teams were empowered to achieve the vision. Although the Technologies division has only been working on these initiatives for a little over three years, they have achieved considerable improvements in customer satisfaction, profitability, and quality. Senior management credits education as the single most important tactic they used to help them improve the competitiveness of their organization.

The United Electric Company is a leading manufacturer of temperature and pressure controls, recorders, and sensors, ranging from thermostats to computer-based multifunction controllers. Founded in 1931, the company has approximately 400 employees. It represents a unique example of how a small company with limited resources can use education as a key tactic for improving organizational effectiveness.

In 1987 the Vice President for Manufacturing, Bruce Hamilton, set a goal for the organization: to become a "world-class" manufacturing company. Realizing that this new approach conflicted with the existing culture, management used education as a tactic to change the culture. They developed a comprehensive program with a strong emphasis on employee empowerment and education. They also eliminated all hourly and salary distinctions, began treating employees as partners, and created a 401K plan to address employees' long-term financial security needs. They called their program, "Education is Action." During its infancy, the program was unstructured, with management buying books on JIT, TQC, SMED (single minute exchange of dies), and Poka-yoke (which is the practice of error-proofing) and encouraging employees to read them. After employees became interested and then enthusiastic about these concepts, a curriculum of education (topics included problem-solving tools, quick changeover, and Poka-yoke) was developed to assist them in operationalizing these concepts in their environment.

Once the employees were armed with the appropriate skills and knowledge, voluntary action centers (a quality circle hybrid) were launched in late 1987 to identify and implement untapped opportunities for improvement. Employees quickly gravitated to this new culture and began to involve themselves actively and to take the initiative in improving the performance of their respective units. Examples of successful projects included elimination of three high-box storage units from the stockroom, conversion of 5,000 square feet of storage for production, elimination of 1,000 inactive parts, and savings of about $25,000 annually in maintenance costs. Other key performance gains since 1987 include:

• Reduction of lead times from 8–12 weeks to 1–2 weeks.

• Decrease in work in process by 80 percent.

• Reduction of finished goods inventory from $1.2 million to $300,000.

• Decrease of stores inventory by 50 percent.

• Increase in on-time deliveries from 65 percent to 95 percent.

The Education is Action program has provided United Electric Company with results that have exceeded their expectations. In addition to significantly improving the organization's competitive position, they were recently awarded the highly prestigious North American Shingo Prize for Manufacturing Excellence.

What do Diamond Star Motors, Digital Equipment Corporation, and the Acme Steel Company have in common? Each has heavily invested in employee education to create a culture of innovation and empowerment. They have used this investment as a springboard for increased organizational performance.

Diamond Star Motors is a joint venture of Chrysler Motor Corporation and Mitsubishi Motors Corporation. This marriage between two giants is mutually advantageous. It has afforded Mitsubishi the opportunity to establish a state-of-the-art manufacturing plant in the United States without incurring a huge financial investment, while allowing Chrysler to learn Japanese manufacturing techniques.

Located south of Chicago, the plant began production of the Plymouth Laser and Mitsubishi Eclipse automobiles in September 1988. The Diamond Star Motors facility has approximately 3,000 employees who are organized into work teams of 10 to 15 cross-trained Associates (the plant uses only two classifications, Production and Maintenance Associates, to promote flexible work rules). All Associates participated in an extensive orientation training program that covered the principles of *Kaizen*, process improvement, problem-solving tools, and group dynamics. Approximately 10 percent of the workforce received training in various Mitsubishi factories throughout Japan.

Digital Equiment Corporation (DEC) is an extremely progressive company that prides itself on successfully introducing cutting-edge technologies and progressive work methods/practices. Through the years they have had considerable success in providing an excellent quality-of-worklife environment for their employees while delivering good financial returns for their investors.

DEC has been at the forefront of new plant designs that incorporate self-directed work teams, JIT, and TQC. This is best exemplified by their Enfield, Connecticut, plant, which employs approximately 250 people. Since beginning operations in the early 1980s, it has been one of the highest-performing plants in DEC based on 21 parameters of cost, quality, and productivity.

DEC management attribute their success to providing extensive education to all employees and developing a culture that facilitates unfiltered communications. Before the plant became operational, DEC invested 18 months in orienting and educating employees. The education spanned a variety of technical and nontechnical areas and targeted all employees throughout the organization. Even after the plant was operational, employees spent an average of one-half day a week educating themselves.

During the last five years the U.S. steel industry has lost billions of dollars. This considerable decline is due to a combination of factors, including: (1) increased foreign competition; (2) lagging technology; (3) an overreliance on vertical integration (companies were heavily integrated, from mining the coal to shipping and forging the steel; when inexpensive sources of domestic coal ran out in the 1950s, the companies chose the most expensive alternative: they continued to mine domestically rather than purchase inexpensive high-grade ore from other countries); (4) falling steel demand (steel was replaced by lighter, less expensive materials such as aluminum, ceramics, and plastics); and (5) volatile labor/management relations (there were a number of prolonged labor stoppages that disrupted supplies to key customers) prompted customers to purchase from more reliable foreign suppliers. In an effort to regain lost market share, the industry has tended to focus on a strategy of quality improvement, cost reductions, and process improvement.

The Acme Steel Company in Illinois has been one of the more encouraging success stories in an industry still groggy from being beaten up by foreign competition. In the early 1980s Acme lost $20 million and was in a perilous financial position. Instead of cutting back the line item most usually reduced during an economic downturn, the education budget, they invested $400,000 to educate employees on the techniques of cost rationalization, productivity improvement, and quality improvement. By the end of the first year of education, they had saved approximately $3 million.

The list of companies that we can add to our success story library is growing on a daily basis. The bottom line is that communications and education are essential ingredients for successful change. Each improves the understanding and commitment of affected stakeholders. True success is not just dependent upon identifying the correct strategy/tactic mix, it also depends upon how well you execute these chosen strategies and tactics. The utilization of a well-thought-out communications strategy and timely and targeted education are the first two key success factors that must be addressed to achieve manufacturing excellence.

Chapter 5

Employee Involvement

The jury is in. Successful change management requires employee involvement and empowerment. The key challenge for many organizations is to correctly identify and to implement the employee involvement program that best supports their initiative. This can be a very difficult process: there are literally hundreds of different types of programs and each program is usually known by one or more acronyms: TEI (total employee involvement), CWI (comprehensive workforce involvement), SWIM (small workgroup improvement management), QC (quality circles). Since many of these programs are slightly different twists on the same theme, it is easy to be overwhelmed by the diversity of choices. Ultimately, the decision comes down to balancing such issues as cost, program sophistication, design/implementation timelines, and resource requirements.

If one performs a comprehensive study of the many employee involvement programs currently in use, it soon becomes obvious that they fall naturally across a continuum (see Figure 5.3 on page 101). On the left end of the continuum the programs tend:

1. *To focus exclusively on solving operational problems.* Individuals or

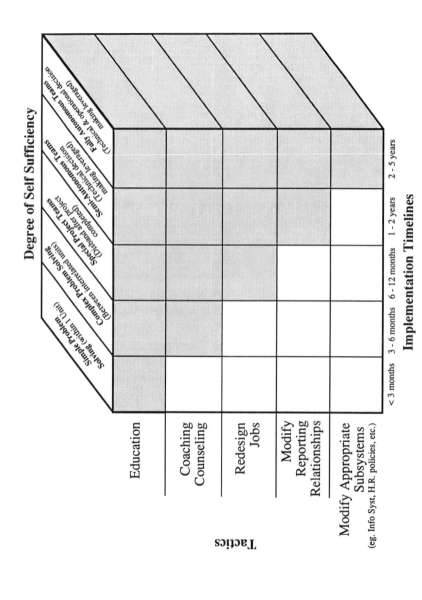

FIGURE 5.1. Implementation timelines for team development.

small groups of employees within a *single* work unit target their efforts on identifying and solving productivity, quality, and cost-related problems that directly impact them. This reactive perspective puts employees in the role of fighting fires instead of preventing them.

2. *To be voluntary, simple, and focused on solving intra-unit problems.* Many sources of variance transcend unit boundaries. Therefore, simple problem solving tends to address the "trivial many" instead of the "critical few" problems. Since these programs are not usually integrated with an organization's vision, strategy, and business objectives, they usually do not support the most important strategic goals facing the organization. This manifests itself in the all too familiar phenomenon in which a group's number one problem is its manager's number ten priority. Although these groups can sometimes demonstrate improvements, more often than not they spend their time chasing the wrong rabbit and produce only small results. Programs at the extreme left side of the continuum also tend to have a structured hierarchy that can require extensive administration and consume significant management and support staff time in meetings. Unwittingly, many of these programs increase overhead costs instead of reducing them. In addition, the programs require little system integration (human resource systems, information systems, etc., are not modified to support the plan).

3. *To produce only incremental results.* The most effective employee involvement programs foster tremendous opportunities for employees to interact. It is through discussions, debate, and conflict that ideas are embellished and true innovation occurs. When an employee merely stuffs a suggestion into the suggestion box, this dynamism does not occur because of the limited opportunities for interaction.

As you progress toward the right side of the continuum, the employee involvement programs increasingly have an entirely different set of characteristics:

1. *The farther along the continuum, the greater the sophistication of the program.* The focus shifts from intragroup problem solving to in-

tergroup problem solving (complex problem solving), and finally to empowering employees to make decisions previously made by management and technical/administrative support groups. Instead of fighting fires, the focus is on getting employees to take initiative and accept responsibility for self-management. This leverage frees up management and technical support people to address higher-level activities.

2. *The probability that an organization will be able to implement a program without outside assistance decreases as you move to the right along the continuum.* The time required to design and implement a program can vary from as little as one week for a suggestion system to three months for a quality circle program. In the case of work teams, it is not uncommon for organizations to invest two to five years of effort before a team is truly self-directed (see Figure 5.1). This complexity is an outgrowth of the amount of systems integration required for success. A company that is contemplating self-directed work teams (SDWT) will have to thoroughly educate the workforce, redesign jobs, modify organizational boundaries, and modify the performance management system to facilitate the transition. These changes require highly specialized skill sets that are not found in most organizations. When available, they are difficult to leverage throughout the organization.

3. *There is a direct relationship between the degree of improvement obtained and the type of program utilized.* We have had the good fortune to observe many different types of employee involvement programs throughout our consulting careers. Most of these programs fall on the left side of the continuum. The chief reason for their popularity is their simplicity. In keeping with the Band-Aid style of management followed by many companies, such programs offer a quick-and-dirty approach to employee involvement. The programs are inexpensive, quick to implement, and provide an out for those who want to create the aura of involvement but still maintain significant control.

Why Do Complex Employee Involvement Programs Provide the Best Results?

The number one asset of any organization is its people. In fact, people are one of the few appreciating assets an organization has. Employee involvement programs on the left end of the continuum tend to isolate employees by focusing and rewarding individual initiative or input. When an employee participates in a suggestion program, he or she is looking at a problem from only one perspective. The real advantage of employee involvement is to focus a *group* of employees with different perspectives on a single objective that supports the organization's *strategic focus*.

When one looks at the cost distribution trends of the manufacturing industry, it becomes even more obvious why employee involvement programs on the right end of the continuum provide greater impact on an organization's competitive position. Figure 5.2 illustrates the cost distribution trends of the *average* manufacturing company since the 1960s. It also forecasts these trends throughout the 1990s. Actual cost distribution trends will vary significantly from company to company, depending on such variables as product mix, technology used, and the like. Close examination of the charts reveals two trends:

1. The direct labor, or "touch content," for the average company has decreased from approximately 40 percent to 10 percent of the overall cost of doing business.

2. Overhead has more than doubled (from 20 percent to 40 percent) and is the largest cost of doing business for most manufacturing companies. Coincidentally, it is also the largest cost for most service organizations. When one analyzes overhead more thoroughly, a startling fact emerges: people are the largest cost driver under overhead. The legions of managers, supervisors, and administrative and technical support staff create the functional silos we have come to accept as a byproduct of American manufacturing. It is frightening to compare the staff size of Mazda's accounts payable department to Ford's: it's about one-third the size! Employee involvement programs on the far right side of the continuum, such as SDWT, significantly reduce overhead. This is achieved by creating self-

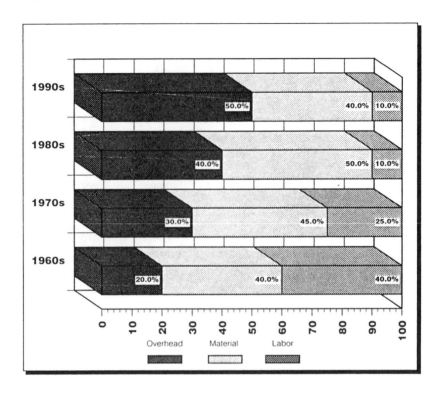

FIGURE 5.2.   Cost distribution trends in U.S. manufacturing.

sufficiency in the workforce through a concerted effort to decentralize appropriate management, administrative, and technical support decision-making responsibilities. This decreases the need for large support staffs and frees up the remaining staff to focus on higher value adding activities.

Commonly Used Types of Employee Involvement Programs

Up to now we have been discussing employee involvement in terms of a theoretical continuum. We now focus our discussion on five employee involvement programs that are commonly used to support the world-class manufacturing initiatives (TQC, JIT, administrative productivity improvement) discussed in Chapter 3. Each program represents a different point along the continuum of Figure 5.3. As we move from left to right on the continuum, the programs are:

1. Suggestion systems.
2. Quality circles.
3. Survey feedback programs.
4. Quality of worklife (QWL) programs.
5. Self-directed work teams (SDWT).

Suggestion Systems

Suggestion systems are one of the oldest and most commonly used types of employee involvement. Their popularity is attributable to the following:

1. They are easy to design and maintain.
2. They require no large investment in training or ongoing program maintenance.
3. They can be used to address problems at the organization, division, or department level.
4. They provide little risk of embarassment to management. Since employees do not directly dialogue with management, volatile issues can easily be sidestepped.

Most suggestion programs include two major components: an administrative control policy (which details who can participate, types of

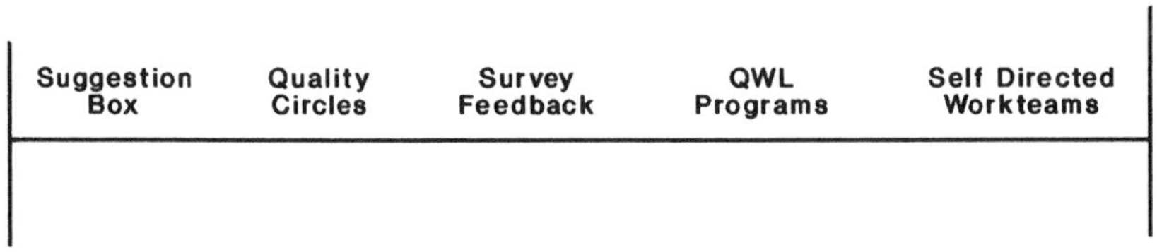

Suggestion Box	Quality Circles	Survey Feedback	QWL Programs	Self Directed Workteams

FIGURE 5.3.   The continuum of employee involvement programs.

reward and recognition, etc.), and several suggestion boxes located strategically within an organization's premises. Although these programs vary in sophistication, most consist of a management or steering committee that has responsibility for reviewing all suggestions received, providing sufficient resources to implement those suggestions it deems most appropriate, and providing legitimacy and management support to the program.

The rationale for implementing a suggestion program seems compelling until one actually takes the time to analyze the historical effectiveness of these programs. The vast majority are really nothing more than social experiments that cultivate the appearance of employee empowerment. In the first two years these programs tend to yield a moderate number of disjointed ideas, most of which have little strategic impact on the overall organization. When employees see only cosmetic changes, their enthusiasm is likely to wane. It's no surprise that so few programs have been running for five or more years. Most are replaced by more sophisticated programs for employee involvement.

Those readers who have suggestion systems in place may be inclined at first to disagree vehemently with our assertions regarding their effectiveness. Typically, when we come into contact with clients who use suggestion systems, they speak about how proud they are of their program. They frequently stress how it instills an *esprit de corps* in the workforce. Others frequently comment on the large number of suggestions that have been received. If we ask how effective the program has been in improving organizational performance, we find there is all too often little long-term quantitative data being collected. Evaluation, if it has been attempted at all, is subjective and is based on general observations or gut feelings.

In our experience, employee suggestion systems have limited utility for the following reasons:

1. Since this type of program does not require extensive employee education on such topics as problem identification, root cause analysis, and solution selection, suggestions commonly address issues of employee dissatisfaction instead of issues that impact organizational performance.

2. Suggestion systems do not require extensive system alignment. This weakens the motivational impact the program exerts on employees.

Since the recognition, performance management, and reward systems are generally not modified to support these programs closely, they may send out a mixed signal to employees. Management may espouse the value of teamwork in the organization's culture but reward individual initiative via the suggestion system—a truly perplexing situation!

Quality Circles

A quality circle is a group of employees, usually 7 to 15 people, from a common work area who meet together, usually on a weekly basis, to identify and solve quality, productivity, and cost-related problems.

Quality circles originated in Japan during the 1950s. Ironically, it was two Americans, W. Edwards Deming and Joseph Juran, who introduced to the Japanese the problem-solving tools and techniques that are the backbone of the quality circle process. During the 1960s the Union of Japanese Scientists and Engineers (JUSE) built upon this earlier statistical training and promoted quality circles throughout Japan. Today it is estimated that more than 75 percent of the corporations in Japan have active quality circle programs. Many identify this employee involvement approach as an essential part of Japan's rise from a low-cost, low-quality producer to an economic powerhouse.

Quality circles are a relatively new approach in the United States. They began to appear in the mid-1970s when Lockheed's Missile System Division and Honeywell first introduced programs in their companies. Their initial successes paved the way for other companies that were looking to mimic some of the Japanese management practices they had read about.

By the late 1970s the quality circle movement was the popular fad for many companies in the aerospace, automotive, steel, and consumer products industries. IBM, TRW, Westinghouse, Digital Equipment Corporation, and Hughes Aircraft all became heavily involved in this technique.

The quality circle structure

Most quality circle programs utilize a multi-tiered structure that clearly establishes roles for all participants. These structures include a steering committee, one or more facilitators, team leaders, and team members.

The steering or advisory committee is usually composed of a vertical cross-section of all employees. It is responsible for:

- Providing direction to the program.
- Promoting the growth of quality circles throughout the organization.
- Selecting a quality circle facilitator.
- Establishing the program's structure (number of circles, how often they meet, etc.).
- Developing administrative control procedures.

The steering committee is usually assisted by one or more quality circle facilitators. Facilitators are responsible for the day-to-day operations of the program. Specifically, they are responsible for identifying and/or delivering any needed education, orienting new team members, coaching team leaders, and making sure each circle has adequate resources. They also administer the recognition program (if one is used) and periodically evaluate the effectiveness of the program.

Each quality circle has a leader. In new programs the supervisor of the work area is usually appointed the circle's first leader. Later, as the circle becomes more cohesive, it is common to rotate other people into this role. The leader is responsible for keeping each of the circles focused on achieving the objectives of the program, assisting other members in applying the problem-solving tools, and maintaining good process interactions.

Membership in a circle is voluntary in most programs. Circle members are empowered to identify problems they want to solve, collect data on the root causes of problems, and make recommendations on how to prevent the problem from recurring. In most programs employees meet on a weekly basis for approximately one hour to apply the structured problem-solving process.

Do quality circles work?

John Deere is a 152-year-old manufacturer of farm, construction, and lawn and grounds care equipment. The company has been mired recently in shrinking agricultural and construction markets and has extremely volatile labor relations.

The Harvester Works plant in Illinois implemented a hybrid quality circles program in the early 1980s. Working closely with the UAW, the company provided a broad base of education for employees and also made a concerted effort to modify their culture. Management improved organizational communications, instituted an open-door policy, and encouraged operators to interface with equipment vendors and customers.

These efforts have paid off handsomely for Deere. After the first year of the program the company realized the following benefits:

- Manufacturing costs were reduced by 30 percent.

- Rejects were reduced by 90 percent.

- Lead times were reduced by 85 percent.

- Prices were cut by 15 to 20 percent.

Beginning in 1985, the Harvester Works plant began enlarging the quality circle program to address interplant issues. Its program focused on improving quality and efficiency and on reducing costs. It encouraged various functional units to communicate more effectively with one another, while motivating employees to accept additional responsibilities.

Honeywell Industries' Automation Systems Division is another example of a company that has had considerable success with quality circles. This division designs and manufactures control systems for refineries, paper mills, and other industrial plants. In 1981 it introduced a modified quality circle program throughout its plant. After the first year it reported the following benefits:

- Thirty percent reduction in production cycle times.

- Ninety-nine percent on-time delivery.

- Nineteen percent reduction in labor costs.

- Thirty-one percent decrease in burden.

- Twenty-five percent improvement in quality.

Survey Feedback Systems

Survey feedback systems are structured, focused employee involvement programs that utilize a data-collection instrument to obtain input from employees on a host of topics ranging from employee attitudes to job satisfaction. The application of surveys to collect data in organizations dates back to the early 1950s when companies such as AT&T, IBM, Ford, and General Motors initially used such instruments to document various job satisfaction indices. Today a high percentage of Fortune 500 companies utilize this approach to assist in planning and implementing organizational change. Organizations use these programs either as a thermometer or as a strategic management tool (see Figure 5.4). Companies that use survey feedback as a thermometer tend to use the process on an irregular basis (whenever there is a crisis) and filter feedback of the results beyond the senior management group. This typically yields short-term fixes and incremental improvements. The more effective programs are well funded and ongoing. In such programs, senior management focuses each level of the hierarchy on the most strategic issues facing the organization. Action plans are then developed and coordinated at the companywide level, division level, and unit level to solve the root cause of the most important problems. Over time, many organizations have developed and shared extensive data bases. This facilitates both normative comparisons (comparing scoring on particular indices to an industry, company, or division average) and trend comparisons (comparing the answers to the same questions over a period of time).

Most survey feedback programs follow these five steps:

1. Identify the objective(s)/success criteria of the program.
2. Conduct education.
3. Design, administer, and tabulate the survey.
4. Feed back results to employees.
5. Conduct cause analysis and develop action plans to solve the root cause of problems.

The first step of any well-designed survey feedback initiative is to identify and confirm the objective of the program. These objectives

Stages

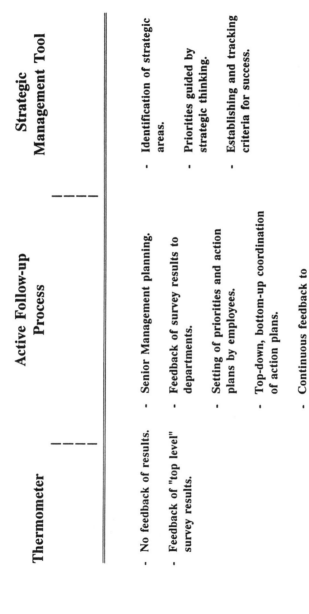

Thermometer	Active Follow-up Process	Strategic Management Tool
- No feedback of results.	- Senior Management planning.	- Identification of strategic areas.
- Feedback of "top level" survey results.	- Feedback of survey results to departments.	- Priorities guided by strategic thinking.
	- Setting of priorities and action plans by employees.	- Establishing and tracking criteria for success.
	- Top-down, bottom-up coordination of action plans.	
	- Continuous feedback to employees.	

FIGURE 5.4. Evolution of the survey process.

By permission of Wm. Schiemann & Associates, Inc.

should closely support the organization's strategy, vision, and operational objectives. Tight linkage of the survey feedback program's objectives to the strategic and operational focus of the organization will enhance the program's impact on improving the competitive position of the company (see Figure 5.5).

Once the objectives have been formalized, a curriculum of education should be developed for all employees who will participate in the program. This education should provide both a conceptual overview of the survey feedback process as well as specific skills needed to design, administer, and evaluate the program. Employees should receive education in root cause analysis, team development skills, and action planning. Managers are typically taught survey tabulation, how to feed back the survey results to their employees, and integrating the action planning process throughout the organization. The better-designed programs tend to emphasize constantly the linkage of the

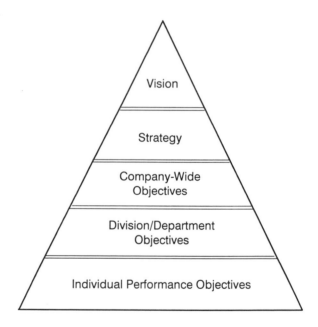

FIGURE 5.5. Strategic considerations in a survey feedback program.

By permission of Wm. Schiemann & Associates, Inc.

survey feedback process to the strategic direction of the organization. This prioritization of effort can be achieved in a number of ways, using a variety of decision criteria. We have developed a strategic prioritization matrix that we have used effectively in a number of client engagements (see Figure 5.6). The matrix can be completed as follows:

Each index (an average of several questions that fall under a common topical category; commonly used indices include rewards for performance, advancement, and innovation) is mapped according to its strategic importance and performance (e.g., how well you scored on the index; was it a strength, a mixed result, or a weakness?). Those indices that fall in the P1 quadrant, high strategic importance and low performing, are the highest priority areas. These areas can then be further prioritized according to their actionability and leveragability. Actionability refers to the degree to which individuals can impact an index. For example, a plant may score low on a rewards-for-performance index but a manager may not have the authority to modify the reward system. Certain indices will impact an organization across a wide range of areas. For example, by improving organizational com-

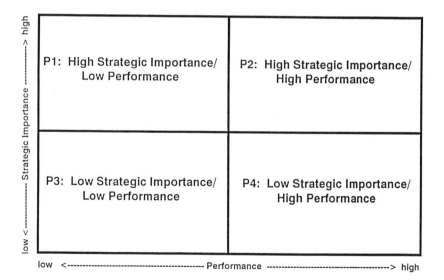

FIGURE 5.6. Strategic prioritization matrix.

By permission of Wm. Schiemann & Associates, Inc.

munications a company may experience positive ripple effects in employee relations, innovation, and job satisfaction. Clearly, communications is a highly leveragable index because it provides considerable bang for the buck.

The logistical issues one must address while undertaking a survey feedback program are enormous. The first Herculean task is the design of the survey instrument. Those programs in which employees from survey locations are involved in the design process tend to outperform those that are designed in a vacuum. Most instruments also include core, custom, and demographic items. Core questions are usually standardized throughout the organization and are focused on the particular objectives of the survey program. Standardization of these questions creates a baseline for conducting a trend analysis over a number of years. It also facilitates the comparison of different organizational units. Custom questions focus on issues that are unique to each particular location. Demographic items facilitate the comparison of results across a potentially wide range of issues (e.g., sex, job category, age).

Once the surveys have been completed, they are tabulated. Reports are usually created and feedback training sessions are held for managers to assist them in presenting those results that are most strategic. This is extremely important because of the length of many of the surveys (100 to 300 questions) currently being used. Employees would be overwhelmed if they were presented with all the data on a 300-question survey.

During the feedback process, the tabulated data are presented to employees. In most instances this is accomplished in a top–down fashion using intact work groups. Once these data are presented, the intact work groups identify the root causes of problems and develop action plans to alleviate them.

Survey feedback at Medico

Medico is a pseudonym for a large pharmaceutical manufacturing company that provides a host of prevention and early-diagnosis products and services to the health care industry. In the early 1980s Medico found itself in a tenuous position: its customer base was deep but too wide. The sales force did not differentiate its efforts and spent too much time on small customers instead of customers with much greater market potential. The existing organization stucture promoted centralized decision making and limited innovation.

In 1987 Medico engaged a consultant to assist it in "turning around" the organization. They utilized a survey feedback program coupled with a focused strategic change management process. The change managment process began with the creation of a vision and mission that clearly described how the newly appointed president wanted the company to evolve. Instead of developing this vision in the safe confines of his office, he spent his first six months getting to know the company by talking to employees. His initial focus was on identifying problems and issues that negatively affected employee satisfaction and organizational performance. A vision statement was then developed and shared with stakeholders to obtain a consensus and confirm the president's understanding of the myriad problems the organization faced. Once the vision was completed, a strategy was developed to achieve the vision.

In 1987 the company began using a survey feedback program to assist it in identifying how well the organization's structure, business systems, people capabilities, and culture supported their strategy. Unlike most survey feedback programs, Medico's was strategically focused. Medico designed a survey instrument that measured the attitudes, dissatisfactions, and perceptions of employees on more than twenty different indices ranging from their level of satisfaction with the company and their job to equity of the performance appraisal and reward systems. The instrument that was created includes over 150 questions, including both core and demographic items, and is administered on an ongoing two-year cycle.

After the survey was administered and tabulated, employees were educated on a wide range of topics related to survey feedback. The survey results were then presented to all employees using a top–down, intact work group model. Root cause analysis was then conducted for the most strategic performance gaps. Action plans were developed to address problems that would be handled at the unit, division, or companywide level.

Over a four-year period the organization has been able to improve significantly on more than 80 percent of the indices measured in the survey. During this time, problems of job satisfaction, employee turnover, employee motivation, and absenteeism have improved. From an operational perspective, volume has more than doubled, profits have increased more than sixfold, and customer responsiveness and satisfaction have considerably increased. These dramatic changes have propelled Medico from the middle of the "pack" to the leadership position in most of the markets they serve.

Quality of Worklife Programs

Labor relations in the United States can best be conceptualized as a roller coaster ride that has several dips and large peaks. Just when you think the ride is smoothing out, you find yourself in an inverted position hanging precariously by your fingertips, fighting for your survival. Since the dawn of the industrial revolution, labor–management relations within the United States may best be described in one word: adversarial! Over the years each side has attempted to maximize its gains at the other's expense.

Perhaps the best way to discuss the evolution of quality of worklife (QWL) programs is to recount key milestones in the evolution of labor–management relations in the United States. In the early 1900s labor unions began to become a prominent way for workers to obtain better treatment, equitable pay, and input into decisions relating to career progression and working conditions. As our country moved from the early days of industrialization, many industries exploited workers, resulting in the widespread growth of unions.

During the 1960s and 1970s, many would say that the pendulum of exploitation swung in the other direction. Unions became so powerful that they began to exert a tremendous influence on organizational decision making. This pressure was most keenly felt by organizations in the areas of wages and benefits. In many instances, gains by workers were out of step with common sense. No longer were people paid according to their skill. Certain job groups, such as automobile assemblers and truck drivers, had inflexible work rules and were not paid according to the criticality of the jobs they performed or the sophistication of the skills they brought to the table. This made it difficult and sometimes impossible for many companies to maintain their competitiveness in an emerging world marketplace.

During the 1970s, a severe recession shook the country. This, in conjunction with the arrival in 1981 of a new Republican administration that gave itself considerable latitude in interpreting and enforcing labor laws, weakened the influence of organized labor. The result was that a growing number of unions across the nation lost protracted strikes. Union power and membership declined markedly during this period. The growing economic role of West Germany, Japan, and several newly industrialized countries adversely affected many manufacturing segments (machine tools, automobiles, steel, etc.) that had been dominated by the United States.

Out of this turmoil grew an awareness by the progressive forces within *both* labor and management that their *mutual* survival was dependent on working toward a more equitable and cooperative relationship. This spawned the beginnings of the QWL movement in the United States. The initial programs were revolutionary because they were designed to improve all aspects of life at work, ranging from pay and working conditions to opportunities for improved career development.

The exact origins of the first QWL programs are a subject of some dispute. Many people believe they are an outgrowth of two events. In the mid-1970s the United Automobile Workers of America (UAW) signed a contract with General Motors Corporation to create cooperative labor–management programs in several plants within General Motors. During this time, the Institute for Social Research at the University of Michigan also began providing subject-matter expertise to a number of organizations interested in implementing QWL programs. As word of the success of these initial programs spread, they became models for other progressive companies to copy and embellish.

Today, QWL programs are commonplace in most of the Fortune 1000 companies. AT&T, Ford, Xerox, and Bethlehem Steel are but a few of the companies with successful programs that focus on improving job satisfaction, opportunities for employee growth, job security, labor–management relations, productivity, and quality. Although these programs vary significantly among themselves in their focus and objectives, most have the following elements:

1. A clearly articulated and defined program organization.
2. A letter of agreement (for unionized locations).
3. A curriculum of specialized education to support the program.

Most of the successful efforts clearly define the program's structure and clarify issues relating to the scope of the program, its objectives, employees covered by the program, the integrating mechanisms to be used to join the labor and management hierarchies. Some programs target groups as small as a manufacturing cell or work team, but most include all employees within a plant. The real challenge is coordinating the different objectives of management and labor within a cogent program that can positively impact organizational performance.

Once the objectives and scope have been agreed upon, a series of committees is usually formed to facilitate communications and organize the efforts of both labor and management. The steering committee is usually the first committee formed. It is commonly composed of local and/or national union leaders and the company's senior managers. The steering committee is typically responsible for providing direction to the program, allocating needed resources, and developing administrative control procedures.

Reporting to the steering committee are one or more action committees that are responsible for data gathering, idea generation, and implementing approved initiatives. These committees, composed of employees, supervisors, and managers, are the "worker bees" that drive the program. It is not uncommon for these action committees to focus on a number of different objectives while operating at multiple levels throughout the organization.

The letter of agreement is the second element common to the more successful QWL programs. This letter, which is signed by both labor and management, is not a part of the normal collective bargaining agreement. It serves to define clearly the joint objectives of the program, to specify the respective roles of labor and management, and to delineate the committee structures. This written document validates the program in the eyes of all impacted stakeholders.

A broad curriculum of education is the backbone of any effective QWL program. These educational programs usually start with a number of seminars that focus on such topics as what a QWL program is, the advantages for labor and management, the objectives of the program, and the expected roles and responsibilities of labor and of management. Advanced education may also address organization assessment, group dynamics, team building, conflict management, problem identification and solving, and communication skills.

Benefits of QWL programs

A variety of benefits can accrue from the successful implementation of a QWL program. Obviously the type and amount of benefits vary depending upon the plan's objectives, scope, and approach. Listed below are the benefits commonly associated with a successful program:

1. *Improved intra/inter-unit communications.* This is an outgrowth of management's becoming more adept at communicating information relating to such things as company profitability, changes in market share, and performance of key benchmark variables. Employees are also more comfortable in communicating their concerns to management in an upward direction.

2. *Better labor–management relations.* Joint objectives and better communications improve the level of trust between labor and management. Instead of being adversaries, both parties begin to view the other as an integral member of the same team.

3. *Improved employee involvement.* QWL programs tend to involve employees in a number of decisions in which they don't usually get a chance to participate. This opportunity for involvement decreases employee resistance to change.

4. *Increased skill development.* QWL programs improve opportunities for skill development through three mechanisms: a curriculum of formalized classroom education, greater opportunities for job rotation, and greater input into the decision-making process.

5. *Improved employee satisfaction.* As changes to the work environment are implemented, employee job satisfaction may increase. This manifests itself in a variety of ways. It is not uncommon for tardiness, absenteeism, and turnover levels to decrease markedly. These indicators correlate with improved employee job satisfaction. Improvements in employee job satisfaction can also carry over to the success of future collective bargaining agreement negotiations. As

employee job satisfaction improves, the negotiation process tends to become more amicable and conciliatory.

QWL at General Motors

General Motors' Tarrytown, New York, car assembly plant is an example of one of the earliest and most successful QWL programs instituted in the United States. It has been the subject of several articles and case studies over the years.

During the late 1960s the Tarrytown plant began to experience alarming declining trends in productivity, employee morale, and employee relations. Labor–management interactions were guarded and extremely adversarial. The plant was dirty, noisy, and overcrowded. An astronomical number of grievances were filed and absenteeism was skyrocketing.

By 1971 the plant had become so uncompetitive it faced the distinct possibility of closing down. With its back to the wall, management decided that the status quo had to be changed. The old game of manufacturing had two sets of rules—one for management and one for labor. Management's rules were simple: follow a "need to know" philosophy and communicate the bare minimum in a top–down fashion, be directive, and use formal authority to get employees to perform the work. The union's rule was to fight management about anything and everything (file grievances over changes in work assignments, work rules, etc.), and fight hard for their constituents, whether they were right or wrong.

Faced with dismal prospects, management approached several senior union officials about a pilot project to redesign the way work was processed in two departments. A joint labor–management committee was formed to design and implement these work design changes. Their approach, loosely based on Socio-Technical Systems Theory, focused on a participatory management style, team-based work flows, and flexible work rules.

Soon after this initial project had been successfully instituted, the approach was expanded throughout the plant. A curriculum of education was developed, and all employees participated in problem solving and human relations seminars. By 1978 the Tarrytown plant had totally reversed itself and became a showcase success within General Motors.

The lessons learned at the Tarrytown plant have been surpassed by a joint venture between General Motors and Toyota called New United Motors Manufacturing Inc. (NUMMI). NUMMI, which is located in Fremont, California, produces the Toyota Corolla, Chevrolet Geo Prism, and Chevrolet Nova. It is the first Japanese-managed auto plant in the United States with a UAW workforce that is paid union wages and benefits. Within its first four years of operation, this plant has achieved productivity and quality levels that exceed anything in the U.S. auto industry and rival Japan's best.

The success of NUMMI is in large part a result of its design, which minimizes levels of management, leverages decision making to the operating workforce (workers are responsible for in-line quality control, line speed, production schedule, etc.), utilizes flexible work rules, and has few job classifications.

In this new design the traditional role of the first-line supervisor has changed from that of autocrat to that of team process facilitator. Management has also made a concerted effort to create an egalitarian culture (management wears the same uniforms as the operating workforce). They also reward employees for taking on additional responsibilities, accepting regular job rotations, and for becoming active members of a work team. In an effort to dispel employees' concerns about working themselves out of a job, management has guaranteed all workers employment security. Their commitment to this promise was tested in 1989 when sales of the Nova slumped. Instead of massive layoffs, the production schedule was reduced by approximately 25 percent and workers were encouraged to participate in a broad battery of educational programs to develop their skills further.

Is NUMMI a success? Most would argue unequivocally yes. The plant has a 50 percent higher productivity level than any other General Motors' plant, while absenteeism is about one-half the GM average. In 1986 MIT conducted a quality audit of NUMMI and rated it 135 out of a possible score of 145. Although several articles have questioned employee satisfaction with this new approach, most employees believe that the current system is more demanding but more equitable. They believe this approach is needed to allow GM to compete more effectively in world markets.

Self-Directed Work Teams

Self-directed work teams (SDWT) are based on an approach called Socio-Technical Systems Theory. Although this approach is considered cutting-edge for U.S. companies, it was created by Eric Trist to explain the research he conducted on the productivity of various British coal mines nearly 40 years ago.

Trist was called in to ascertain why the productivity of coal mines fell when state-of-the-art technology replaced small teams of miners who worked with hand tools. Trist found that the least productive mines had the following characteristics:

1. Miners performed repetitive, highly structured tasks.
2. Workers were closely supervised by management. They were told what to do, when to do it, and how to do it.
3. Employees were highly specialized and performed only a small piece of the overall task.

(Although Trist identified these characteristics by studying coal mining, they remind us of many manufacturing companies with which we have worked.)

Trist realized that there was an inverse relationship between the amount and sophistication of the technology used and employee job satisfaction. The most productive environments were those that (1) balanced technology while allowing workers to actualize their needs for autonomy (employees were fully responsible for their own work); (2) had jobs with considerable task significance (individuals were responsible for completing a whole task rather than a series of small, fractured subtasks); (3) had jobs with significant task variety (they fostered the opportunity to learn new skills continually); (4) had jobs with task importance (a perception that the task is important and meaningful); and (5) provide ongoing feedback (being able to know how one is doing on a regular basis) relative to job performance.

The redesign of jobs around intact work teams is an important employee involvement technique that can be used to assist organizations in implementing change. It represents the extreme right end of the employee involvement continuum we discussed earlier. Although it is the most difficult type of employee involvement program to implement, it usually provides the most significant positive impacts.

Characteristics of SDWT

An SDWT is a small group of individuals (usually fewer than 20 people) who are given responsibility for planning and executing a whole meaningful piece of work (e.g., manufacture a whole product or subassembly). This innovative employee involvement approach has been used effectively by organizations in the manufacturing, retail, and financial services industries. It is also known by a variety of other names: autonomous work groups, self-managing teams, high-involvement teams, and superteams. The more successful programs tend to follow a similar design model (see Figure 5.7) and include the following five elements:

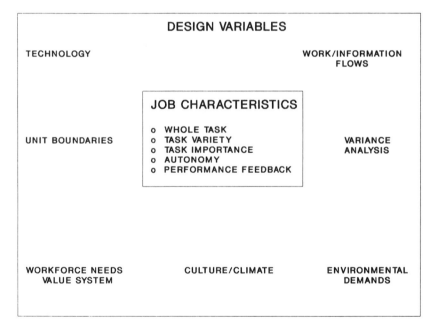

FIGURE 5.7. **Design model for self-directed work teams.**

1. Work is redesigned around a team that is physically located in the same area and is responsible for performing a complete task.

2. Through a combination of education and job rotation, team members are cross-trained in a variety of skills relative to the team's core task.

3. Team members have responsibility for a number of upstream and downstream functions, as well as supervisory and support responsibilities. Typical responsiblities assumed by an SDWT can include work scheduling, job assignments, material handling, preventive maintenance, housekeeping, record keeping, improving work methods, educating other team members, setup, assembly/fabrication, and safety. Many of the more successful programs also leverage human resource responsibilities down to the team. These responsibilities can include employee selection, performance appraisal, progressive discipline, termination, salary determinations, and career progression.

4. The team operates in an environment with well-defined physical and task boundaries. This maximizes the interdependence of all team members and fosters social interactions.

5. Jobs are redesigned so that team members get immediate feedback on their performance, and have sufficient autonomy and decision-making authority to manage their own outcomes.

Self-directed work teams have become a popular employee involvement and job redesign approach because traditional organization designs have created persistent problems for management over the years. Traditional designs tend: (1) to centralize decision making, slowing down the response to changes in the market (e.g., limited operational flexibility, poor customer satisfaction); (2) to create narrowly defined jobs with rigid work rules that tend to foster insufficient intra/ interunit cooperation, inhibit innovation, and promote low job satisfaction; (3) to foster large management and staff support functions (high overhead).

Self-directed work teams at Lake Superior Paper Industries

In 1987 the Lake Superior Paper Industries (LSPI) opened up a greenfield mill in Minnesota to manufacture supercalendered paper and polished uncoated paper that is used in many newspapers, supplements, catalogs, and magazines. This state-of-the-art mill was designed to optimize social resources and technical resources (technology used, work flows, job redesign, etc.) given the demands the environment places on the organization (see Figure 5.8). The LSPI mill employs approximately 350 people and is an outgrowth of a joint venture between Minnesota Power and Light and Pentair Inc. It was specifically designed to support an overall world-class manufacturing initiative with three areas of focus: productivity improvement, quality improvement, and safety.

Plant design. The Lake Superior Paper Industries mill was designed using a structured top–down approach. During the mill's conceptual design, senior management formed a transition team that was charged with turning an untried method into a fully functioning manufacturing facility. Utilizing an outside consultant, they focused their initial at-

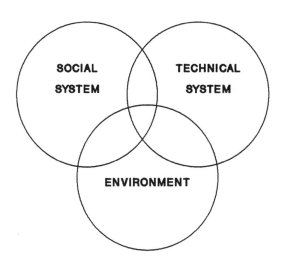

FIGURE 5.8. **Balancing the three systems at LSPI.**

tention on educating themselves in the principles behind self-directed work teams, visited other plants that were designed using the Socio-Technical Systems approach, and participated in a variety of educational activities. During this process they developed numerous iterations of the plant's physical layout, work flows, and organizational structure.

Once satisfied with their design, senior management began the staffing-up process by hiring several team managers who completed seminars on communications, conflict management, and meeting management. Once this education was completed, a number of production employees were hired to work on the fourteen teams that operated on a twelve-hour rotating shift schedule.

As the teams completed their education, they were expected to take on progressively more administrative, supervisory, and production responsibilities. The goal for each team was full self-sufficiency and responsibility for the following:

- Work schedules.
- Starting times.
- Career advancement.
- Work assignments.
- Vacation planning.
- Hiring and transferring employees.
- Employee development.
- Team goals.
- Equipment maintenance.
- Management of overtime.

An integral part of the self-directed work team approach was a skill-based-pay reward system that covered most administrative and production employees. The plan based salary progression on the acquisition of technical and social skills. Employees had the opportunity to progress through the following four pay levels:

Level 1: All new hires with no industry experience.

Level 2: Basic mill knowledge/skills; also completed orientation and safety education.

Level 3: Certified in one skill block.

Level 4: Able to demonstrate various levels of leadership skills.

Benefits. During its initial eighteen months of full operation, the mill has achieved the following results:

1. Instead of incurring a projected $17 million loss, it made $3 million profit.
2. Actual shipments exceeded planned shipments by 20 percent.
3. The mill consistently exceeded industry and company standards regarding safety.
4. Absenteeism was approximately one-fifth the industry average.
5. Job lots fell from 16 percent to approximately 4 percent.

In this chapter we have discussed the importance of employee involvement in implementing change, and have outlined five specific programs that fall along the involvement continuum. Employee involvement is not an option or an afterthought; care must be exercised to identify which type of program will best support the strategies, tactics, and initiatives upon which you are embarking.

It is also important to reiterate that employee involvement programs are not static but evolve over time. Regardless of where your program falls along the continuum, a well-designed employee involvement initiative will mature and move progressively to the right of the continuum. The most effective programs are those that focus on leveraging decision making to ameliorate the organization's true cost drivers. This will improve operational flexibility and maximize the value added each employee contributes.

Total Systems Integration

An organization is similar in many ways to the human body. Both monitor and respond to stimuli in the outside environment and both are composed of a number of subsystems. The human body is composed of the skeletal system, the nervous system, the circulatory system, and so on. Organizations are similarly composed of subsystems such as the information system, the human resource system, and the planning or goal-setting system. Effective long-term change requires the integration and coordination of all an organization's subsystems to support an initiative closely. Every time the status quo is modified, each of the subsystems within the organization may be affected.

In this chapter we discuss the fourth key success factor for managing change: systems integration. Although there are a number of subsystems within an organization, by far the most important to address when implementing change are the human resource systems. These systems have the greatest impact on employee attitudes, actions, and behaviors. We therefore focus most of our discussion in this chapter on how change affects the human resource systems. It is important, however, that one not forget to address the other organizational subsystems when undertaking a change project. Perhaps the best way to explain the concept and importance of systems integration is by example. Since we earlier proposed that manufacturing companies need to adopt three strategies—JIT, TQC, and administrative productivity improvement—to compete successfully in the 1990s, we discuss the concept of systems integration using examples from these strategies.

Common System Integration Issues in Implementing JIT

One of the critical errors often made when implementing JIT is ignoring how it will impact the existing reward system. Whichever way you slice it, JIT means more work for employees. Instead of just being asked to load and unload a piece of equipment, employees are now *required* to take on a number of additional responsibilities ranging from material handling and engineering support to setup and preventive maintenance. Unless employees are compensated for taking on these additional responsibilities, the initiative is likely to encounter strong employee resistance.

Figure 6.1 depicts the behaviors and performance measures that are most frequently used in traditional and world-class manufacturing environments. In a traditional environment the behaviors usually rewarded include compliance to management directives, maintenance of the status quo, skill specialization, and individual initiative. The performance measures most commonly used are machine utilization and

Traditional Environment	WCM Environment
Behaviors:	**Behaviors:**
Specialization	Multi-Skill Competence
Individual Accountability	Obligation to Group Goals
Work Independently	Work as Part of a Team
Performance Measures:	**Performance Measures:**
Machine Utilization	Quality
Worker Efficiency	Number of Employee Innovations
Individual Output	Output of Cell/Team

FIGURE 6.1.   Comparison of traditional and WCM environments.

worker efficiency. Clearly, the focus is on maximizing speed and minimizing unit cost. Companies that are implementing JIT in an effort to achieve world-class performance should be rewarding such behaviors as self-regulation, willingness to work as part of a team, and flexibility in accepting job assignments. The performance measures that should be used range from tracking quality and output of the cell to exact attainment of schedule.

It suddenly becomes clear why, after initial success, so many JIT initiatives screech to a grinding halt. The behaviors and performance measures in a traditional environment are almost exactly *opposite* those you would want to reward in a JIT environment. Since human behavior tends to be self-satisfying, it is imperative to modify the existing reward system early in the transition process.

Two types of reward systems most closely support a JIT transition. These reward systems are skill-based pay (SBP) and productivity gainsharing. SPB is a reward system that bases salary levels on the variety and complexity of skills an employee possesses, while gainsharing is a *bonus*-based reward system that rewards team output. These reward systems can be used either as stand-alones or in combination.

In most cases an SBP plan should be implemented first because it rewards employee flexibility and will have a greater impact on employee attitudes and behaviors. In this instance flexibility means broad work rules, multi-skilling, and cooperation. Cooperation within groups is essential for cellular manufacturing, quick changeover teams, and small group improvement activities (SGIA). SBP also rewards cooperation among formally isolated functional groups. This is necessary to balance the resources in the transition from the "functional factory" into a focused factory. Since production is synchronized to the demand rate in a JIT environment, it is inappropriate to optimize machine utilization or worker efficiency. This would build excess inventory and contribute to the need for additional storage space or material handling. Productivity gainsharing is appropriate because it rewards group output and synchronizes the output of all the operations in the cell.

An organization's people systems are the fuel that moves the JIT transition forward. These systems are powerfully influenced by the appropriateness of the recognition and reward system being used. Often forgotten is a basic premise regarding motivation: If you want an individual to alter behavior or work habits, there has to be either an encouragement for doing so (reward) or a tangible (and recognized) penalty for noncompliance. Traditional reward systems provide neither reward nor punishment. In many instances traditional reward systems—those appropriate to a before-JIT environment—may have been the reason why the new JIT approach was desirable; the traditional practices or people system "ways" got us to where we are! Why would we expect those same systems to provide us with the recognition and reward mechanisms that will take us where we want to be in a new JIT environment?

Since most managers who undertake a JIT initiative fall under the operations umbrella, they frequently lack conceptual or hands-on experience regarding gainsharing and SBP reward systems. Therefore, we believe, an in-depth discussion of SBP and gainsharing reward systems will be of value to the reader.

Skill-Based Pay

Skill-based pay is a pay-for-performance reward and recognition system that promotes workforce flexibility by rewarding individuals on the basis of the number, type, and depth of skills mastered. It is significantly different from the other reward systems commonly used throughout the manufacturing industry. It is not unusual for traditional reward systems to have twenty or more different job classifications (the greater the number of classifications, the less flexible the workforce), rigid work rules, and jobs where employees perform mundane, repetitive tasks. Feedback mechanisms that are utilized tend to be formal (the supervisor appraises performance once per year) and not integrated with career and salary progression. SBP reward systems base salary on the depth and breadth of jobs an employee can *perform*. Since SBP provides employees an incentive to become generalists, most SBP systems reward flexible work rules. Companies that utilize SBP redesign jobs to leverage decision-making authority over those tasks that are able to provide the greatest positive impact on the bottom line. By reducing the key cost drivers of the business and enlarging jobs, employee flexibility is maximized.

Skill-based pay systems have been in use since the late 1970s. These systems have been designed to cover a diverse cross-section of employees, ranging from hourly production workers to exempt professional groups. As merit-based reward systems, they avoid most of the traps found in seniority-based plans. The jury is in on the step systems, found in many manufacturing companies, that base career and salary progression solely on seniority: they simply don't work! These systems promote mediocrity because employees have little incentive to surpass spoken or unspoken performance expectations. What results is a population of employees who persevere because their high need for security has been all but assured. Under these step systems, seniority is the driving force, not performance; therefore, it is extremely difficult to identify and coach/counsel low-performing employees. This tends to frustrate individuals who have high career aspirations—the "fast trackers." They are forced either to scale back their expectations or to look for employment opportunities with a more progressive company.

SBP reward systems are also known by a variety of other names, such as pay-for-knowledge reward systems, knowledge-based compensation plans, multi-skill compensation systems, and multi-job pay plans. Regardless of the name, all SBP plans are based on one philosophy: the more you *learn*, the more you *earn*. It is to the successful *application* of specific skills that salary and career progression are tied.

Skill-based pay systems have been implemented successfully in process, repetitive, and job shop manufacturing environments. Although they are not a panacea for addressing all of the inequities in an organization's people systems, they have been implemented in a number of companies such as General Foods, Proctor and Gamble, Westinghouse, Shell Canada, TRW, Digital Equipment Corporation, General Motors, Vitramon Inc., and Anheuser Busch. It is no coincidence that the companies that have had significant experience in productivity improvement also have had the most practice and success in implementing SBP reward systems. Successful plans tend to include the following components:

- A job rotation system that facilitates employee skill diversification.

- An employee involvement program that focuses on leveraging the decision-making responsibility for those tasks that will provide the greatest source of competitive advantage (focus is usually on reducing cycle times and/or operating costs).

- A well-designed curriculum that specifies the classroom and on-the-job education needed for each skill block/job covered by the plan.
- A structured skill evaluation process that is based on objective, job-related criteria. This is used to certify and recertify skill acquisition.

Types of Plans

Skill-based pay systems can be categorized by the types of skills tracked and rewarded. There are five types of SBP systems commonly used today:

1. *Vertical skill systems* measure the acquisition of input or output skills within *one* job or skill block. For example, a wave solder equipment operator may learn how to perform equipment changeover, preventive maintenance, or inspection.
2. *Horizontal skill systems* reward employees for learning skills that *transcend different* jobs or skill blocks. An example of a horizontal skill system would be rewarding a lathe operator for learning how to operate a drill press or deburring machine.
3. *Administrative skill systems* measure and reward the acquisition of administrative skills. It is not uncommon for cells that are designed using the self-directed work team approach to leverage decision making for purchasing, work scheduling, job scheduling, and the like to team members.
4. *Basic skill systems* reward employees for the acquisition of such basic skills as four-function math, eighth-grade reading proficiency, and fluency in speaking English. Although infrequently used, basic skill systems are expected to become popular in the near future as the workforce accommodates a large number of workers who lack basic skills proficiency and speak English as a second language.
5. As the name implies, *combination systems* utilize two or more of the first four systems.

Skill Levels

Skill-based pay systems vary in the number and sequencing of the skills an employee can decide to learn and master. Most plans reward employees by the number of different skills mastered within a work group. After having their skill mastery certified, employees are encouraged to join another group and learn the skills required for that group. Some programs place a cap on the number of skills an employee can learn while others encourage employees to master all of the skills needed in the entire plant. The greater the number of skills an employee can learn, the greater the challenge of testing and maintaining skill proficiency.

Several of the more sophisticated systems require employees to learn a minimum number of skills as a requirement for future employment. Some programs also establish a minimum time period to stay in a job (say, three to six months) after becoming certified. This allows the organization to recoup education costs and offset decreases in productivity due to the learning curves associated with job rotation.

Skill Mastery

Most successful SBP plans utilize a structured process to measure skill mastery. The onus of evaluation usually falls on either the supervisor, an evaluation committee, or a peer review process. Certification of skill mastery is usually accomplished either through observation, by oral or written tests, or through demonstrated job performance. Depending on the scope and sophistication of the program, it is not uncommon to require all employees to have their skill mastery recertified to maintain existing salary levels. Many established systems have quotas on the number of employees who can be at a given skill/pay level at one time.

Effect on Pay Classifications

Typically, SBP plans utilize fewer than five job classifications, each requiring several incremental steps. This skill step progression eliminates rigid work rules, eases the administration of the plan, and facilitates the cross-training of the workforce.

Pay progression can be conceptualized through the following scenario: John Smith has been hired to fill a vacancy in the ABCDE subassembly cell. This cell is composed of five physically linked operations. As an entry-level operator he is paid the market rate of $8.00 per hour and is responsible initially for the operation of machine A. From this starting point he has the opportunity to learn setup, inspection, and preventive maintenance on machine A. After a combination of on-the-job training, coaching, possible classroom education, and work experience, John demonstrates skill mastery of Operation 1. He then receives a nominal pay increase and is rotated to Operation 2. This process of rotation, training, demonstration of skill mastery, and incremental pay increases is repeated until he reaches the highest skill level specified in the administrative control procedures (see Figure 6.2).

Advantages

Organizations that utilize SBP systems frequently cite the following advantages for both the organization and the employees:

Organizational perspective

1. Employees understand the overall business much better. This is an outgrowth of the job rotation system and SGIA programs.
2. Employee problem-solving capabilities are improved. The structured job rotation system allows employees to understand upstream and downstream operations. This facilitates the identification and elimination of nonvalued activities.
3. Manufacturing flexibility is improved. A key objective of JIT is to maximize overall manufacturing flexibility. True manufacturing flexibility is an outgrowth of improvement in both operational and employee flexibility. By reducing lot sizes, reducing setup times, and developing focused production operations, operational flexibility is improved. Once this occurs, it is necessary to maximize employee flexibility by creating a self-sufficient and multiskilled workforce.
4. Overhead is reduced. Because decision-making responsibility is leveraged down within the organization, employees do not need the amount of support found in conventionally designed manufacturing companies. This affords the organization the opportunity to reduce significantly the staffing levels of managers, supervisors, and support personnel.

EQUIPMENT OPERATOR	SKILL LEVELS MACHINE GROUP 1					MACHINE GROUP 2		
	HORIZONTAL PROGRESSION							
	OPERATIONS							
	1	2	3	4	5	1	2	3
VERTICAL PROGRESSION	MACHINE A OPERATE	MACHINE B OPERATE	MACHINE C OPERATE	MACHINE D OPERATE	MACHINE E OPERATE			
	SET UP A	SET UP B	SET UP C	SET UP D	SET UP E			
	CHECK OUT AND INSPECTION A	CHECK OUT AND INSPECTION B	CHECK OUT AND INSPECTION C	CHECK OUT AND INSPECTION D	CHECK OUT AND INSPECTION E			
	NORMAL PREVENTIVE MAINTENANCE A	NORMAL PREVENTIVE MAINTENANCE B	NORMAL PREVENTIVE MAINTENANCE C	NORMAL PREVENTIVE MAINTENANCE D	NORMAL PREVENTIVE MAINTENANCE E			

FIGURE 6.2.   Sample skill-progression matrix.

133

Employee perspective

1. Job satisfaction and challenge are improved. This is an outgrowth of redesigning jobs to give employees greater opportunities for learning, greater task variability, and more responsibility.
2. Job security for the operating workforce is improved. Since organizations are able to leverage significant amounts of technical and supervisory decision making, they tend to be lean. When a business downturn occurs, they are less likely to displace employees.
3. There is opportunity for more frequent pay increases. Successful SBP plans address the unique needs of all employees because career progression and salary increases are a function of each employee's ability and motivation level.

Implementation Issues

Organizations that are masters at responding to changes in their external environment realize that the successful implementation of an innovation, such as an SBP system, requires significant upfront analysis to determine the "degree of fit." Therefore, any company that is contemplating an SBP system should embark on an organizational assessment that focuses on analyzing potential impacts on key subsystems (information system, other human resource policies and procedures, etc.), assessing compatibility with the existing cultural characteristics, and soliciting labor/union input at the earliest opportunity.

Since SBP is so new, we will present a broad ten-task process for designing and implementing an SBP plan that is applicable to most organizations (see Figure 6.3).

> *Task 1:* Establish Project Organization. During this initial task, a management advisory group is established to provide direction to the project, approve deliverables, and ensure cross- functional commitment to the project. Once this group has been established, a charter is created that clearly defines the role and limits of decision making authority for the design team. The design team, composed

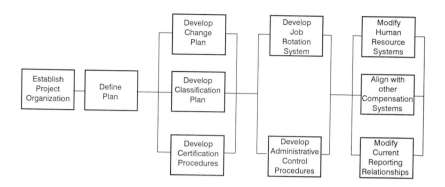

FIGURE 6.3.   Designing and implementing an SBP plan.

of a vertical cross-section of the organization, is responsible for the day-to-day project management activities.

Task 2: Define the Plan. This task begins with the creation of objectives for the SBP plan. Once the plan is finalized, it is important to conduct an in-depth analysis of work methods and process flows. Natural separations in the way work is processed soon become obvious, as well as which groups of employees should be covered by the plan. Once these factors are finalized, jobs are redesigned and appropriate responsibilities are then leveraged to the workforce.

Task 3: Develop Change Plan. Effective change plans often include a commitment strategy and a communication strategy. The commitment strategy identifies which groups of employees must support SBP to ensure success and identifies any outstanding issues or concerns. These matters must be addressed in the design of the SBP plan. The communication strategy specifies what will be communicated to each group of employees and how it will be communicated, and also identifies mechanisms for soliciting input.

Task 4: Develop Classification System. Once the boundaries of the plan have been defined, pay grades are developed. This is accomplished by identifying compensable factors for each job and developing a job classification system.

Task 5: Develop Certification Procedures. Evaluation procedures are developed that identify who is responsible for measuring skill mastery, how skills will be measured, and appropriate evaluation criteria for each job.

Task 6: Develop Job Rotation System. A rotation system should be designed either to interface with an existing Human Resources Information System or, depending on the size of the organization, to be administrated manually. An integral component of this system is a comprehensive curriculum plan. This plan should sequence the technical and nontechnical education needed for each skill block. On-the-job and classroom education is then developed and sequenced.

Task 7: Develop Administrative Control Procedures. Once the SBP plan has been conceptually designed, it is important to develop administrative control procedures that clearly detail the boundaries of the plan. Issues that are frequently addressed range from specifying the minimum number of jobs that must be mastered to topping out.

Task 8: Modify Human Resource Systems. At this point in the implementation, all Human Resource systems (e.g., transfer, orientation, employee selection) are reviewed and, if necessary, revised to support the SBP transition more closely.

Task 9: Align with Other Compensation Systems. In order to institutionalize SBP throughout the organization, it is important to align all other compensation systems (especially those that reward supervisors and managers) to support the SBP plan.

Task 10: Modify Current Reporting Relationships. The final step in the implementation process is to review the current reporting relationships and increase spans of control where applicable. This step usually occurs after the system has been operational for an extended period of time and is a normal outgrowth of having multiskilled employees who require less supervision.

Skill-Based Pay at Ceramco

Company background

Ceramco is a pseudonym for a subsidiary of a Fortune 500, publicly held company with its headquarters in the Northeast. Founded in the 1940s, it is a high-tech manufacturer of precise ceramic and porcelain capacitors. Ceramco's products are used extensively in the telecommunications, computer, automotive, military/space, and medical electronics industries.

Plan description

In response to a large backlog of orders and forecasts indicating that their business would experience significant growth, Ceramco began construction of a new plant in Virginia in late 1987. This factory of the future was designed to incorporate many of the tactics being utilized by world-class companies.

In 1989 Ceramco engaged a consultant to assist it in designing and implementing an SBP reward system. The SBP project consisted of two phases that occurred over a nine-month period.

Phase I: plan design. During the initial phase a project organization was established to provide direction to the initiative and to oversee day-to-day project tasks. Education in SBP concepts was conducted and the following design objectives for the plan were formulated:

1. To promote a lean management-to-staff ratio.
2. To support a low direct-labor-to-technical-support ratio.
3. To maximize employee multi-skill competence.
4. To optimize employee job satisfaction.

An in-depth work flow and task analysis was conducted to identify the jobs that lent themselves most readily to the SBP plan. Jobs were then redesigned to leverage decision making over such things as quality, preventive maintenance, material handling, and fabrication. The jobs or skill blocks were then arranged into three work groups and a structured path of skill progression was developed for each group (see Figure 6.4). Once this was agreed upon, objective skill certification criteria were developed and a curriculum of education was created to assist in new-skill acquisition.

Phase II: plantwide implementation. Employee implementation teams were established to facilitate the rollout of the SBP plan. The plan was evaluated on an ongoing basis by comparing key benchmark measures

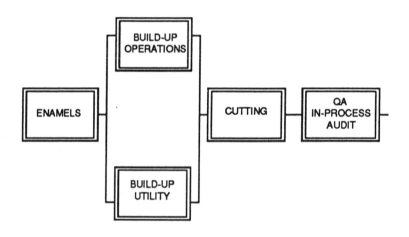

SKILL PROGRESSION

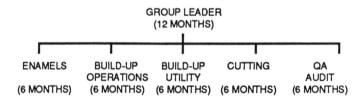

FIGURE 6.4.   Process flow and skill progression in a typical work group.

to the plan's interim and terminal objectives. As the plan matured, modifications were made to the certification criteria and skill progression sequence.

Results

After the first year of operations, Ceramco evaluated its SBP program. The company had achieved the following results:

1. Absenteeism, turnover, and tardiness were well below the industry and company average.
2. The plant required only four technical support personnel and four managers to support a workforce of 200 employees. This reduced their overhead as measured in dollars to 70 percent of the company average.
3. Fifty percent of the workforce was certified in two or more skill blocks.
4. On-time delivery was 25 percent better than the company average.

Productivity Gainsharing

Gainsharing is a term used to describe any group bonus and employee involvement plan that rewards employees for improving group productivity. It compares performance in a current work period to a baseline. These baselines are developed either by using engineering standards or through historical records of performance. Any time employees improve upon the baseline a percentage of the gains is shared with them according to a predetermined formula.

Since productivity gainsharing plans are bonus systems, they require a base salary structure. This base salary structure must maintain internal equity (within the company, pay relationships between different jobs should be equitable) and external equity (pay rates for each job should be comparable to the market rate in the company's geographic area).

As the phrase suggests, productivity gainsharing plans reward improvements in productivity. Although productivity can be measured in many different ways, it is usually calculated as a ratio of outputs to inputs. A measurable increase in productivity is usually the result of one of the following two scenarios:

1. Greater production output with equal or less resource input, or
2. Equal production output with less resource input.

Virtually all of the successful gainsharing programs in use utilize clearly written and communicated objectives. These objectives are linked to the organization's strategic and business plan. For optimum results, the plan objectives should closely support the key success factors of the business. For example, if one of the key success factors is quality, the program should focus on improving some aspect of quality, such as reducing scrap. The variability of plan objectives falls across a continuum from those companies that emphasize reducing energy consumption to those that focus on reducing direct labor hours and material usage.

Since gainsharing plans have been in existence in one form or another since the 1930s, there is a large amount of evidence to show that these approaches are logically sound, and work. Organizations that have implemented plans report the following operational and quality of worklife (QWL) benefits:

Operational Benefits

- Improved utilization of capital, labor, materials, or energy.
- Improved quality and productivity.
- Improved problem-solving capability.
- Increased organizational flexibility.
- More efficient production methods.

QWL Benefits

- Reductions in turnover, absenteeism, and tardiness.
- Improved job satisfaction.
- Improved cross-functional cooperation.
- Better labor–management relations.

• Increased employee involvement.

The U.S. General Accounting Office (GAO) recently conducted a study of a cross-section of organizations in the nonprofit, financial services, and manufacturing industries that have implemented gain-sharing programs. The objective of this study was to identify the various types of gainsharing plans in place and to identify benefits obtained to date; these were the results:

1. Firms that had gainsharing plans in operation for five or more years averaged almost 29 percent savings in labor cost. Organizations that had plans in operation for less than five years averaged savings of 8.5 percent.
2. Of the organizations reported, 80 percent experienced improved labor relations, 47.2 percent reported fewer grievances, and 36.1 percent reported less absenteeism and turnover.

Profit Sharing versus Gainsharing

Profit sharing is not the same thing as gainsharing (see Figure 6.5). Although the plans have been successfully implemented side by side, a growing body of evidence suggests that gainsharing provides a great-

Plan Variables	Profit Sharing	Gainsharing
Employees covered	All employees	Variable
Philosophy	Pay for performance (Vesting requirements)	Pay for performance
Flexibility	Minimally flexible	Highly flexible
Frequency of payout	Quarterly, yearly	Usually monthly
Formula	Based on allocation of pre-tax earnings	Financial/physical
Motivational impact	Marginal to moderate	Moderate to excellent

FIGURE 6.5. Comparison of gainsharing and profit-sharing plans.

er impact on the operational peformance of the host organization. An analysis of variables for each plan reveals several striking dissimilarities:

1. Most profit-sharing plans cover all employees within the physical location of a plant or office. Some even utilize one plan to cover all employees within the company. Gainsharing programs vary significantly with regard to the populations of employees who are covered by the plan. Depending on the measurement formula used, it is not uncommon to have several plans within a plant, positioned around either product groups (focus factories) or functions. Gainsharing plans offer the flexibility to cover a population of employees within a work unit or the entire plant.

2. Although both profit-sharing and gainsharing plans are characterized as pay for performance, profit-sharing plans usually have lengthy vesting requirements. It is not uncommon for employees to have to wait several years before being fully vested in the company's contribution. Gainsharing plans usually have no vesting requirement but may impose a waiting period before employees are able to participate. The rationale behind this is that newly hired employees usually face some learning curve. While in this learning mode, they are theoretically not contributing as much to operational performance as their colleagues. After employees are fully competent in their respective operations, they are allowed to participate in the program.

3. Profit-sharing plans are not as flexible as gainsharing plans. The former are usually based on a formula that allocates a percentage of pre- or post-tax earnings to employees. This is usually determined at the beginning of each year by either the board of directors or senior management. Gainsharing plans are based on formulas that track the ratio of outputs to inputs. These formulas can be modified as needed for a variety of reasons, ranging from changes in product mix to technological or capital improvements.

4. Profit-sharing plans tend to have a weaker impact on the bottom line and do not typically motivate employees. Since most profit-sharing plans pay out on a yearly basis, too much time may have elapsed between effort and reward. Behavioral scientists have ar-

gued for years that the most effective type of reward system closely links the efforts of employees to a valued reward. This creates a problem in most organizations because there are usually several groups of employees (secretaries, accountants, etc.) for whom it is quite difficult to measure the effect of their efforts on organizational performance. Well-designed gainsharing plans cover only those employees who can directly influence the outcomes for which they are held accountable.

Types of Plans

Four different types of gainsharing plans are commonly used today: the Scanlon plan, the Rucker plan, Improshare, and custom plans. The key differences between the plans lie in the way in which the bonus is calculated and in the amount and type of employee involvement that is required.

The Scanlon plan was developed in 1935 by Joseph Scanlon, an employee of the financially troubled Empire Steel and Tin Company. Initially, the plan was designed as an involvement program to solicit employee input in solving production problems. A bonus provision was added later.

As the oldest and most widely used type of gainsharing, this sophisticated program promotes job enrichment, workforce involvement, and productivity improvement. Since the plan is based on the historical ratio of labor cost to sales value of production, it is particularly appropriate for companies that have a high "touch labor" content because it rewards improvements in labor savings.

Allen W. Rucker, an economist, developed the Rucker gainsharing plan in the 1930s. Rucker noted that the ratio of labor costs to production value was historically stable for approximately 90 percent of manufacturing companies. Subsequent studies have confirmed the continuation of this trend to the present time. This principle became the underlying tenet behind the Rucker plan, which measures productivity by tracking the amount of value added to a product.

Because the Rucker plan utilizes a more sophisticated measurement formula, it can track labor, materials, energy, and the cost of purchased services. It is therefore a much more useful approach for companies that want to measure and reward improvements in a wide range of variables. Using the traditional Rucker formula, employees could therefore obtain a bonus payout for:

- Reducing usage of materials or supplies.
- Improving output per man-hour.
- Improving quality.
- Improving production methods.
- Improving safety performance.

Mitchell Fein, an industrial engineer, developed Improshare (IMproved PROductivity through SHARing) in 1974. The goal of this program is to produce more output with fewer labor hours. Unlike the Scanlon and Rucker plans, Improshare utilizes a physical formula that rewards improvement in the ratio of finished goods to the actual man-hours required for production. Bonuses are a function of the number of hours saved for a given number of units produced compared to a historical production standard; they are paid weekly, and productivity improvements are usually shared equally.

Since many of the gainsharing plans in use today are based on the prevailing wisdom of the 1930s, many companies find that the textbook approach of these plans simply does not work in their environment. Typically these companies create their own customized plans which utilize more sophisticated means of worker involvement (e.g., self-directed work teams) or create a specialized measurement formula to fit their needs more closely.

Features of Each Plan

Employees covered

Gainsharing plans vary markedly with regard to the employee groups that they cover. Some plans cover all employees (more common in Improshare) while others cover either hourly production workers (Scanlon plan) or all employees except senior management (Rucker plan). A good rule of thumb to follow when deciding who should be covered by the plan is to include *only* those employees who can most directly impact the variables in the measurement formula. Gainsharing cannot be used as a means to rectify a lack of internal pay equity among employee groups. There are, however, groups of employees who fall into grey areas. This makes the equitable disposition of these employee groups a challenge. For example, a common problem revolves around whether to include the first-line supervisors in the plan. If they are not included, salary compression may occur; if supervisors are included, conflict may result because production workers may not feel that supervisors should share in productivity gains that were an outgrowth of their efforts.

Types of measurement formulas

There are two distinct types of gainsharing measurement formulas:

1. *Physical formulas* reward employees for improving the relationship between physical units of output and input. This type of formula is used in Improshare plans. Organizations that opt for physical formulas have plan objectives that focus on rewarding employees on the basis of variables that are directly within their control. (Physical formulas are only indirectly affected by changes in selling prices or market conditions.) These formulas are very popular because they are easily understood and the results are directly controllable by employees. Unfortunately, they can also theoretically pay bonuses during periods of declining or nonexistent profitability.

2. The Rucker and Scanlon plans utilize *financial formulas*. Organizations that use these formulas seek to tie employee bonuses to overall organizational performance. A trade-off when using financial formulas is that they are affected by factors (such as poor management decisions or market changes) that are beyond the control of the target population and thus may have an adverse effect on employee motivation and commitment. Although these formulas provide a more global measurement of the state of an organization's performance, they are usually much more difficult for employees to understand.

The Scanlon formula

Most Scanlon plans calculate their base ratio by dividing predetermined payroll costs by the value of production. Thus, employees receive a bonus in any month when the actual labor costs are less than the established base ratio. For example, if the base ratio is 10 percent and the value of production (sales plus or minus inventory) equals $100,000, then the allowed labor equals $10,000. If the actual labor utilized was $7,000, then a bonus pool of $3,000 is generated. Depending on the plan guidelines, a percentage would then be allocated to management for capital expenditures and the rest allocated to employees (minus any deficit reserve).

The Rucker formula

The Rucker plan uses a financial formula to calculate the value-added of production. Once this has been completed, the Rucker Standard is calculated. This standard usually represents the historical ratio of labor, materials, supplies, purchased services, and energy to the value-added of production. Bonuses are paid in any month when actual expenses are less than the Rucker Standard. See Figure 6.6 for an example of the Rucker calculations.

The Improshare formula

A key component of the Improshare formula is the establishment of a baseline. Since most plants produce multiple product lines, a measurement base must be established that reflects the past average productivity for all products and for the entire plant. In most production facilities the total hours worked are much higher than the time allotted through production standards. (This is due to the fact that production time standards usually do not include nonproductive work such as preventive maintenance, setups, scrap, and salvage.) A base productivity factor (BPF) must be calculated to convert engineering standards to reflect the previous year's productivity and to factor in all nonproductive time. The BPF is computed by dividing the total production and nonproduction hours by the facility's total hours worked.

The dynamics of the Improshare plan are most easily explained

1. VALUE OF PRODUCTION (SALES +/- INVENTORY CHANGES, ALLOWANCES ETC.)	$1,000,000

2. ACTUAL EXPENSES

A. LABOR	$100,000
B. MATERIALS & SUPPLIES	500,000
C. PURCHASED SERVICES	50,000
D. ENERGY	20,000
	670,000

3. RUCKER STANDARD (65% OF VALUE OF PRODUCTION)	650,000
4. GAIN	20,000
5. DEFICIT RESERVE	6,000
6. BONUS PAYOUT	14,000

FIGURE 6.6.   Sample Rucker plan calculation.

through an example. Suppose a single-product plant with 200 employees produces 100,000 units of XYZ product. If the employees work 50 weeks, or 200,000 hours, their average time per unit is 2 hours (200,000/100,000). If during a week 200 employees work 8,000 hours and produce 4,500 units, the value of the output will be 4,500 units × 2.0 hours per unit, or 9,000 hours. The gain would be 9,000 − 8,000 hours, or 1,000 hours. In a traditional Improshare plan, 50 percent of the savings in excess of the standard would be shared by all employees. This would mean 500/8,000, or 6.25 percent, added to each employee's weekly pay.

The baseline

Baselines are used as a starting point to calculate improvements. They are developed either by using historical data (the average level of a variable is tracked over a time period ranging from six months to five years), through corporate goal setting (for organizations that encounter frequent innovations and cannot make use of historical baselines), or by engineering measurement.

Organizations can use either fixed, adjustable, rolling, or targeted baselines. Fixed baselines remain constant during the plan's lifetime. This provides employees with an added advantage because their bonuses reflect improvements made in previous periods. Adjustable baselines are revised periodically (usually annually) to the level of performance achieved in the previous base period. Plans that utilize adjustable baselines frequently encounter problems in maintaining bonus levels because employees must constantly generate new improvements. Rolling baselines calculate the average performance for a specific number of periods. The length used typically varies from four to six weeks. For example, if a company utilizes a four-week rolling average as it begins the first week of month two, the first week of month one is dropped. Targeted baselines are used when no appropriate baselines are available. This can occur when a new product or technology is introduced or when manufacturing processes are changed significantly and the old baselines are no longer valid.

The bonus payout

The percentage of savings shared with employees varies with the type of plan and its objectives. In general, plans that measure only labor productivity share the greatest percentage of savings with employees. The Scanlon plan (labor-only formula) traditionally returns 75 percent of any gains to employees. Multicost systems (Rucker plan) usually pay out between 25 and 50 percent of the savings to employees. Improshare usually splits savings on a 50/50 basis with employees.

When determining the bonus share, management should consider the capital intensity of the business, frequency of baseline changes, and expected motivational impact. Capital-intensive industries generally pay out a smaller share to employees. Plans that frequently change the baseline typically provide employees with a larger share.

Organizations can divide the employees' share of gains as follows:

1. Percent of income: the bonus pool is translated into a percentage of salaries with each employee receiving an *equal percentage* of payout. This method is used in about 75 percent of the plans.
2. Equal shares: every employee receives the *same absolute dollar amount*.

3. Hours worked: the bonus is paid in terms of *dollars per hour worked* and applied to individual employees accordingly.

Bonuses are paid out either weekly, monthly, quarterly, or annually. Most plans utilize a monthly payout. When deciding on payout frequency, one should consider availability of data (reporting systems capabilities), motivational intent desired (in general, the greater the frequency, the greater the impact), administrative costs (the more frequent the payout, the greater the administrative costs), and the level of environmental uncertainty (uncertainty in the environment can result in wide payout variations).

Deficit reserve

A deficit reserve is sometimes used to link bonus payout to company performance. It protects a company from paying out excessive bonuses during periods of slumping profitability. It also acts as a cushion against year-end adjustments to accounting data.

In most plans employees contribute between 15 and 40 percent of their bonus to a deficit reserve account. Any money left in the account at the end of the year is paid out to employees. Organizations that do not utilize deficit reserve accounts base their bonuses on the average of several periods of performance.

Deficit reserve accounts are frequently used in Scanlon and Rucker gainsharing plans. An example that illustrates how a deficit reserve account works is found in column 1 of Figure 6.7. During period 1,

		POSITIVE BALANCE	NEGATIVE BALANCE
1.	NET SALES	$500,000	$500,000
2.	INV. VARIATION	50,000	50,000
3.	VALUE OF PROD.	550,000	550,000
4.	ALLOWABLE EXPENSE (75% OF #3)	412,500	412,500
5.	ACTUAL EXPENSES	400,000	420,000
6.	GAIN/LOSS	+12,500	-7,500
7.	BONUS POOL (70% OF #6)	8,750	0
8.	PAYROLL	100,000	100,000
9.	BONUS % (#7/#8)	8.75%	0
10.	DEFICIT RESERVE	2,625	0
11.	PREVIOUS RESERVE	10,000	10,000
12.	RESERVE TO DATE	12,625	4,750

FIGURE 6.7.   Deficit reserve calculation.

actual expenses ($400,000) were less than the baseline or allowed expenses ($412,500). This resulted in a *net gain* of $8,750 (70 percent of the difference between actual and allowed expenses), which was available for distribution to employees. The remaining 30 percent ($2,625) would be added to the previous reserve balance of $10,000, making a new balance of $12,625. Column 2 is an example in which the actual expenses exceed the baseline or allowable expenses. In this scenario, a loss of $7,500 has occurred during a work period. Seventy percent of this loss ($5,250) is deducted from the previous reserve balance of $10,000, the new balance thus being $4,750.

Deficit reserve accounts in a sense spread the risk between management and employees. When performance exceeds the baseline, both stakeholders receive a "bonus." When performance is below the baseline, both parties lose.

Employee involvement

The type and amount of employee involvement used to support the various gainsharing programs vary widely. While employee involvement programs are important components of both the Scanlon and the Rucker plans, they are not required for Improshare plans. There is some evidence which suggests that those Improshare plans that do have an employee involvement component outperform those that do not.

The primary focus of the employee involvement plan is to build synergy between interdependent work units and to facilitate process improvement. This supports the overall philosophy of gainsharing: to help employees work smarter, not harder.

The Scanlon and Rucker plans use similar employee involvement approaches. The Scanlon plan utilizes a three-tiered employee involvement program composed of a screening committeee, a production committee, and a suggestion system (see Figure 6.8). The Rucker plan employs a two-tiered approach that uses both a plantwide suggestion system and production committees.

The screening committee is usually composed of union representatives, functional department heads, members from each production team, and operational supervisors. Half the members of this committee are usually elected by the employees, while the other half are appointed by management. The purpose of this committee is to help the pro-

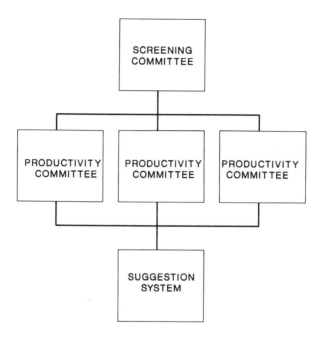

FIGURE 6.8. Scanlon plan employee involvement hierarchy.

duction teams focus on which issues to work on, provide information on operational problems, handle decisions that exceed the level of authority for the production teams, and periodically to review the bonus payout.

Production committees are created for each unit covered by the plan. Committees are composed of the department foreman or supervisor and several elected workers who meet on a monthly basis. The committee members are responsible for analyzing, evaluating, and implementing suggestions that solely affect their unit and cost less than a prescribed amount. Suggestions that relate to other units or that involve additional budget expenditures are referred to the plantwide screening committee.

Suggestion systems are frequently used as an adjunct to the employee involvement committee structure. The suggestions usually become an input into the discussions that occur within the production committees.

With this conceptual overview of the three gainsharing plans, we now present a case study on each plan to illustrate how the plans were instrumental in supporting operational change initiatives.

The Scanlon Plan at ElectroCo

Company background

ElectroCo is a pseudonym for a small, privately held manufacturing company located in the Midwest. Since its founding in the late 1960s it has supplied a variety of electronic components to the automobile and high-tech defense industries. ElectroCo employs 125 people and has annual sales in excess of 25 million dollars.

Plan characteristics

ElectroCo installed a modified Scanlon plan in 1983 to support a Total Quality initiative. Prior to this time, most direct-labor employees were on a piecework incentive system. This caused ongoing bickering around such issues as job selection and equity of standards. It also contributed significantly to the company's high overhead expense.

ElectroCo's Scanlon plan covers all hourly direct and indirect employees. The key components of the plan include the standard Scanlon formula and a deficit reserve account. Productivity improvements are split 50/50 between the employees and the company.

Employee involvement is organized around a structured quality circles approach. Participation in the problem-solving process is voluntary and is focused exclusively on solving production-related problems. A formal employee involvement policy was developed that addresses a host of administrative issues ranging from the roles and responsibilities of employees to the limits of employee decision authority.

Results

ElectroCo has assessed the effectiveness of its Scanlon plan on an annual basis. The company reports the following benefits since the program's inception:

1. The number of suggestions per employee has increased by 300 percent.

2. Absenteeism, turnover, and tardiness have continually declined and are now below industry standards.

3. Productivity has increased at an average annual rate of 10 percent.

4. The cost of products sold as a percentage of the sales price has remained fairly constant.

The Rucker Plan at GearCo

Company background

GearCo is a pseudonym for a large Midwestern manufacturer of gears, speed reducers, and gear boxes. Founded in 1951, this Fortune 500 company employs more than 50,000 people worldwide and has annual sales in excess of 3 billion dollars.

Plan description

In the late 1970s GearCo began to experience increased competition from foreign manufacturers that eroded significant portions of the company's market share. GearCo's 800-person unionized plant in Illinois was hit extremely hard by this business downturn. In 1977 this plant had a major strike. Shortly thereafter, management recognized the need to improve work conditions, improve productivity, and increase employee involvement in decision making. During the next two years a joint labor–management committee was formed to identify initiatives that could improve plant operations while responding to the needs of employees. The consensus of the committee was to implement a Rucker productivity gainsharing program. This recommendation was quickly approved by management and in early 1979 the company engaged an outside consultant to assist it. In June of 1979, the Rucker plan was installed. It covered all employees except senior management, included a quality circle employee involvement program, and utilized a traditional Rucker formula. Bonuses were paid out in a check separate from the regular payroll and distributed on a monthly basis. The plan used a deficit reserve account and any balance left in the reserve was distributed to the plan participants at the end of the year.

Results

GearCo just completed a five-year review of its Rucker Plan, with the following results:

1. The number of grievances filed decreased by 38 percent.
2. Turnover declined by 40 percent.
3. Absenteeism decreased by 25 percent.
4. Productivity increased by 21 percent.
5. Positive bonuses were paid out an average of ten times per year with bonuses ranging from 5 to 15 percent of employee pay.

Improshare at EnerCo

Company background

EnerCo is a pseudonym for a small, privately held energy equipment corporation located in the Southwest. Founded in the early 1900s, this company employs 500 people and is composed of four divisions that manufacture a wide range of products from crane blocks and wellheads to a variety of forgings. During its eighty years of existence, the company's culture has always remained paternalistic, nurturing, and egalitarian. EnerCo has a long history of involving employees in decision making and in sharing profits with employees.

Program description

During the mid-1970s, management and employees alike became unhappy with the annual bonus system that had been in place for the past 20 years. Management believed this system was not providing them with the source of competitive advantage they desired, while employees wanted more frequent payouts and a system that they felt was directly tied to their efforts.

In the summer of 1979 EnerCo engaged a consultant to design a productivity gainsharing plan for their organization. After an assessment it was decided that Improshare was the most appropriate gainsharing system for EnerCo. In December of 1979, a modified Improshare plan was introduced. The plan covered all direct-labor, quality control, materials, and maintenance personnel. The base productivity factor was selected after a careful analysis using past organization performance data to model how different factors would affect the bonus. The plan paid weekly bonuses based on the plant's performance during the preceding two months. Any bonuses to which the employees were entitled were paid out in a separate check. Payouts were based on a 50/50 share of all productivity improvements.

Results

According to the company's V.P. for Operations, the plan has achieved the following results over the last five years:

1. Turnover and absenteeism have decreased by 20 percent.
2. A cooperative attitude has developed among interdependent units.
3. The company shipped 25 percent more product.

Other Human Resource Considerations

We have discussed in this chapter the importance of modifying the reward system to closely support various initiatives. We have presented an overview of skill-based pay as a potential base salary reward system and have discussed productivity gainsharing as a potential bonus-based reward system.

Unfortunately, the integration of an organization's Human Resource system starts—it does not end—with the successful design and implementation of a reward system. We spend so much of our efforts in addressing this because the reward system is the single most important factor that affects employee attitudes and behavior. It is also critical for creating the culture that will most closely support the attainment of business objectives. In order to achieve total Human Resources integration, an analysis of all of the HR policies, procedures, programs, and systems must be undertaken. The HR systems that are commonly affected during JIT, Total Quality, and administrative productivity improvement transitions are:

- Recognition system.
- New hire orientation policy.
- Performance appraisal policy for managers, supervisors, and the operating workforce.
- Employee selection procedures and selection criteria.
- Human resource information system.
- Promotion, transfer, and job posting policies.
- Seniority privileges policy.
- Termination policy.
- Discipline policy.
- Collective bargaining agreement (number of job classifications, work rules, etc.).
- Reward/bonus systems for managers and professional support staff.
- Employee involvement program.
- Internal educational programs.

The analysis and modification of these systems is a time-consuming process that requires long lead times, senior management commitment, and a sponsor with extensive political acumen. This last trait is needed because many of the systems mentioned above are imposed or heavily controlled from the corporate headquarters. Exemption or significant modification of these policies can be an arduous process.

It is also important to reiterate that, in addition to the human resource systems, there are several other subsystems (planning and goal setting, information system, etc.) that are likely to be affected by these initiatives. True systems integration requires an assessment to determine how these various systems are affected and then the development of a plan to modify *each* system to support the change initiative.

Chapter $$7$$

How to Apply the Concepts

The last several chapters in this book have presented a conceptual framework for a company to achieve world-class manufacturing performance. We have identified and discussed the key success factors required to institutionalize JIT, TQC, and administrative productivity improvement within an organization. We now would like to present a structured "how-to" approach for applying the concepts to any of these initiatives. Our approach is based on a field-tested methodology that we have used successfully in our consulting practice. By combining this methodology, which addresses the "people" side of change, with the conventional workplans that focus on the technical aspects of each initiative, the probability of success is greatly increased.

Over the last several years a number of articles have described companies that have achieved "textbook" results when implementing organizational change. A careful analysis of the approaches used by these companies reveals a common thread. Success depends to a large extent on utilizing a balanced approach that identifies how the change will impact an organization's technical, business, and people management systems. Once the scope and severity of impacts on these systems were identified, they were modified to closely support the change. Conversely, if one studies the approach used by the vast majority of

157

organizations that achieved only incremental results, one finds that a common oversight has been made in that management focused virtually all of its time, effort, and resources on the technical aspects of the initiative (e.g., redesigning physical layouts, reducing lot sizes, reducing setup times).

A Conceptual Overview of the Change Management Process

Figure 7.1 depicts a conceptual model of the dynamics of organizational change. The model is composed of three concentric rectangles. The outermost rectangle depicts the common events or change drivers that tend to motivate companies to "bite the bullet" and undertake an initiative. Except for a handful of very progressive companies (which are already excellent and want to become outstanding), most organizations will pursue an initiative only when one or more of the change drivers in their environment provide an opportunity or threat significant enough to necessitate their action. The list of variables that can drive change is, perhaps, endless. Some are industry-specific while others are company- or market-specific. Based on our experiences, the most common change drivers range from increased foreign or domestic competition (e.g., incursion of Japanese, European, or other U.S. entrants) and pressure from stockholders (e.g., falling stock prices, smaller dividends) to pressures from the labor unions (labor–management committees designed to improve QWL conditions).

The middle rectangle includes the organizational subsystems that are commonly impacted by a change initiative. The degree of impact depends on a number of issues, ranging from the type of initiative planned and the scope of introduction to the size of the organization. Ultimately, those subsystems that are impacted must be aligned to support closely the requirements of the change initiative.

The innermost rectangle identifies the elements that are required to bring about effective change. Organizations are composed of people. Since people tend to be creatures of habit, change forces them to give up what is known and to embrace something that is relatively unknown and possibly threatening. In order for this to happpen throughout an

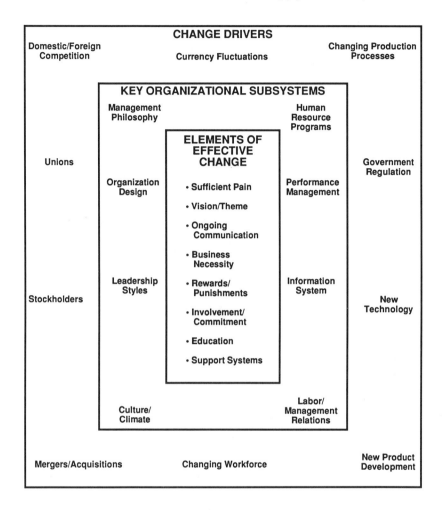

FIGURE 7.1.   A model for organizational change.

organization, management must make a conscious effort to increase the *pain* of maintaining the status quo. Only when the pain of maintaining the status quo becomes stronger than the pain of accepting change will an initiative be institutionalized. The key role for management is therefore to increase the pain.

The change process can be conceptualized as an evolutionary process composed of the following three phases: the existing state, one or more transitions, and the desired state (see Figure 7.2). Management's sole objective during this first phase should be to increase dissatisfaction with the existing conditions. This can be accomplished by increasing the visibility of the threat or crisis (the driver behind the change) so that it becomes real and a sense of urgency is felt throughout the organization. Other tactics include communicating a concise theme or vision to all stakeholders, utilizing three-way communications, using a mix of appropriate rewards and punishments, and involving all affected groups in the design/implementation process.

Effort must also be expended to motivate all stakeholders to support the initiative actively. This can be accomplished by stressing the benefits of the change and by utilizing role models throughout the organization ("walk the talk") to demonstrate management commitment to the initiative and to address latent concerns (fears of future competence, job security, etc.) from each stakeholder group. It is important to be aware of and to acknowledge publicly any groups of stakeholders who will be negatively impacted. By being truthful and setting expectations realistically, management can reduce resistance. The combination of these tactics will in most cases provide the impetus needed to move the organization from the existing state through one or more milestone transitions.

The objective during the transition phase should be to implement the change in one or more stages; this eases project management and allows employees time to adjust to the change. It is important to realize

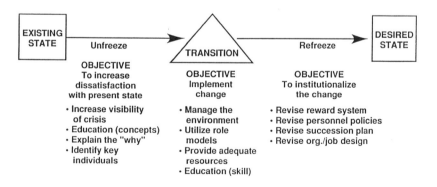

FIGURE 7.2.   The three phases of organizational change.

early that organizations and people have a limited capacity to accept change. They can assimilate only a certain amount of change within a limited period of time. When planning an initiative, it is important to follow an old Asian proverb, "The best way to eat an elephant is one bite at a time." Better to err on the side of conservatism, rather than risk the success of the entire project by moving too quickly.

We recently had the opportunity to work with a Fortune 100 company that simultaneously undertook initiatives in world-class manufacturing, self-directed work teams, a workforce transition project, and total employee involvement. Although each initiative was theoretically sound, the company encountered overt and covert forms of resistance because they overwhelmed employees by trying to accomplish too much too soon.

The primary objective of the third phase is to institutionalize the change throughout the organization. During this final stage, the recently introduced initiative becomes the new status quo. This is where the ball is frequently fumbled. It is imperative at this point to focus on the people systems and to effect modifications to the reward system, human resource policies and procedures, and performance management systems.

Steps in Planning and Implementing Change

Figure 7.3 is an illustration of the change management methodology that we have integrated into our consulting practice. It was developed

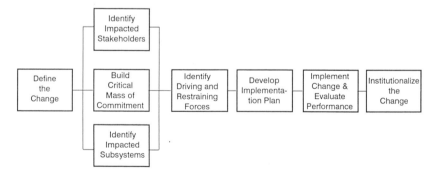

FIGURE 7.3. The eight tasks of any change initiative.

as an outgrowth of our work with, and observation of, world-class companies in Japan, Europe, and the United States.

The change planning and implementation process consists of the following eight tasks, each of which is discussed in turn:

1. Define the change.
2. Identify impacted stakeholders.
3. Build a critical mass of commitment.
4. Identify impacted subsystems.
5. Identify driving and restraining forces.
6. Develop an implementation plan.
7. Implement change and evaluate performance periodically.
8. Institutionalize the change.

It is important to note that, as the figure indicates, some of the tasks are completed sequentially while others are completed concurrently. Depending on the organization and the type of initiative being undertaken, the sequence of tasks may also differ.

Task 1: Define the Change

This beginning task consists of three key steps: defining the existing state, creating a vision, and designing and facilitating strategic and tactical education.

Defining the existing state means developing a detailed description of the current state of affairs, including the need for change (what's broken). At this early stage, it is important to develop valid, objective baselines. These baselines should provide an accurate picture of the current level of organizational performance. For an accurate measurement of progress, the baselines used should measure and track financial, operational, and quality of worklife variables. Listed below are some baselines commonly associated with an administrative productivity improvement program. It is important to note that the baselines ultimately selected must be customized for each organization and each change initiative.

Financial Baselines

- Sales per employee.
- Assets per employee.
- Working capital employed.
- Cost of quality.

Operational Baselines

- Quality levels.
- Cycle times.
- Bottlenecks.
- Management-to-staff ratio.

QWL Baselines

- Job satisfaction.
- Relationships with peers, supervisor.
- Turnover, absenteeism, tardiness.
- Number of grievances.

Although using QWL baselines to measure employee response to the change may seem obvious, this is rarely done, perhaps in part because of a lack of personnel who have skills in survey development and administration (this is how QWL baselines are usually measured). Most companies measure success solely on the basis of improvements in financial and operational baselines. It is no wonder that so many initiatives encounter significant employee resistance, require longer-than-expected implementation timelines, and never achieve a critical mass of commitment.

Once the baselines have been developed, it is important to create a detailed vision of the desired end state. The vision should be specific enough to identify any attitude, value, or behavior change that is expected. It may also state the interim and terminal objectives, which can facilitate ongoing project management later on. The final vision statement should be detailed enough to create a picture of what the change looks like in the minds of all stakeholders. When finished, it should be one of the first documents communicated to all employees.

Listed below are the other critical issues that should be communicated to the appropriate stakeholders:

- The business necessity behind the change.
- Timelines, approach, and key milestones.
- What will and what will not change.
- Who will be affected.
- How impacted employees will be affected.
- The benefits from an organizational and employee perspective.

Once employees understand the vision, it is important to identify and conduct any needed education. In most cases this education is conducted in a top–down fashion, following the guidelines discussed in Chapter 4. For example, in a Total Quality program, the education may initially cover such topics as the characteristics of future competition, what is Total Quality, Total Quality strategies, and design/implementation variables. Benchmarking can also be used to compare the company quantitatively with its competitors across a wide range of key success factors. Benchmarking can be used to compare products, process capabilities (cycle times for key processes, customer service levels, etc.), or even financial results. In addition to being used as an educational tool, benchmarking can be used effectively to create dissatisfaction with the present state and to create a sense of urgency to change.

Using a Total Quality example, as education is broadened throughout the organization it should focus less on conceptual or strategic issues and more on new skill acquisition. This second tier of education should be targeted to all impacted stakeholders, especially individuals in focal roles (key positions within an organization that must support the initiative for it to be successful). This education should focus on behavior modification as well as technical and nontechnical skill acquisition.

First-line supervisors play one of the most important focal roles in any Total Quality transition. Unfortunately, management does not usually allocate sufficient resources to educating them on how their role will change as Total Quality becomes engrained within the organization. The result is role confusion and skill deficiency.

In order for Total Quality to be successful, the traditional supervisor's role typically should change from one that is directive and autocratic to one of empowering the operating workforce to actively support the continuous improvement process. To facilitate the empowerment process, the supervisors' role must radically change to focusing on obtaining the necessary resources for their work units and on being coaches, and facilitators. Education is the key to bringing about this transition. The education that is usually provided for these employee groups is myopically focused on such technical areas as statistical process control, process improvement, and designing visual controls. These "hard" side areas are undoubtedly important, but without training in such "soft" areas as participatory management, coaching, and team building and conflict management, behavior change is unlikely to occur.

Task 2: Identify Impacted Stakeholders

An organization is interdependent with its external environment. It is therefore important to identify how a change initiative will impact *all* stakeholders.

Figure 7.4 depicts an example of a completed stakeholder analysis worksheet for a JIT initiative. (Note that it does not identify the entire spectrum of stakeholders who can potentially be impacted by the program, nor does it analyze the impacts in the degree of detail needed for a real-world application.) A stakeholder analysis can be used to:

1. Identify which groups of stakeholders both within and outside of the organization will be affected by the change program.

2. Identify the type and severity of impact, also to identify possible responses the project team can undertake to deal equitably with each stakeholder group.

3. Identify the existing interdependencies or demands each stakeholder places on the organization.

4. Assess how the change initiative will affect these interdependencies.

Focal Roles	Impacts/Concerns	Potential Responses
Suppliers	Pressure to manufacture in smaller lots Increased operational flexibility Shorter lead time Improved quality	Encourage management from suppliers to visit our company to learn about JIT Train suppliers Provide technical assistance
Employees	How will JIT impact: - job security - wage/benefit package - security privileges - work rules	Guarantee employment security Buyout existing incentive system Provide training Encourage employees to visit other companies that utilize JIT

FIGURE 7.4.   JIT stakeholder analysis worksheet.

A stakeholder analysis includes the following four steps: (1) brainstorm a list of all stakeholders; (2) identify the demands they currently make on the organization; (3) determine how the change will impact the stakeholders and identify their concerns; (4) prioritize a list of possible responses to address each stakeholder's impacts and concerns.

When completing a stakeholder analysis, it is important to involve a vertical cross-section of employees to obtain the best data. In Figure 7.4 we have identified two stakeholder groups (suppliers and employees).

Let us take a closer look at how two of the stakeholder groups—suppliers and the operating workforce—can be impacted during a JIT transition. The demands most companies make on their suppliers are smaller lots, more frequent deliveries, greater flexibility, shorter lead times, and improved quality. The host company may even require they adopt JIT as a condition for future business. Suppliers will probably be concerned about being displaced as the vendor base is reduced. In an effort to address the concerns of suppliers equitably, the host company has a range of possible responses that might include: allowing the operating management of key suppliers to visit their plant periodically during the transition; offering JIT education to key vendor personnel; or offering technical assistance to aid suppliers in their own JIT transition.

The demands the operating workforce can place on an organization can include improved job security, wage and benefit increases, and protection of seniority privileges. As an organization makes the transition to JIT, the operating workforce may have serious concerns about taking on more responsibility, about equitable compensation, and about fear of job displacement. Possible responses might include a buyout of the existing piece-rate incentive system (which contradicts the essence of JIT) and studying the feasibility of introducing an SBP reward system. Management might also consider developing a policy that guarantees employment security, alleviating possible employee fears about losing a job because of improvements in productivity.

Task 3: Build a Critical Mass of Commitment

Critical mass is a function of the number of people supporting the change, their level of commitment, and the adequacy of their skills. There are three distinct tactics that can be used to build this critical mass of commitment: structural integration, environmental management, and individual integration.

Structural integration is the process of obtaining cascading commitment throughout the organization. Cascading commitment is a matter of getting enough people at *each* level in the hierarchy to accept the role of either champion or missionary. It is not uncommon for an individual to take on more than one role at any given time. A champion or missionary can also be a member of a larger group of employees who are impacted by the change.

"Champions" are defined as those people who have the position power (formal authority, rank, title, etc.) to authorize change to occur. That is, by the nature of their status within an organization, they can mandate change.

"Missionaries" are those individuals who are willing to roll up their sleeves and actively assist in implementing the initiative. Whenever possible, it is a good strategy to utilize informal group leaders to act as missionaries. Since these individuals have tremendous credibility among the workforce, making use of them will significantly reduce resistance while improving the communication process.

Once these internal change agents are selected, they should be educated thoroughly in both the technical aspects relative to the change initiative, as well as a variety of organization development (OD) skills. The OD skills required may include:

- Organization assessment.
- Conflict management.
- Team building.
- Process consultation.
- Job or organization design.
- Project management.
- Change management.

"Impacted groups" are those groups of individuals who are *directly* affected by the change. In most initiatives such as JIT the impacted groups are further broken down into primary and secondary groupings. The primary impacted groups in a JIT program tend to be the operating workforce, first-line supervisors, and technical support groups. Since the JIT transition usually begins on the shop floor, these groups must be committed to the project at its inception. When the JIT initiative expands beyond the shop floor areas, additional effort must be expended on obtaining the commitment of all secondary impacted groups (such as Sales, Marketing, Customer Service, Quality Control, and Purchasing).

There are several principles that must be followed when using the structural integration strategy. First and foremost, successful large-scale organizational change occurs *only* in a top–down fashion. We define large-scale change as any initiative that impacts multiple functions or organizational subsystems and requires significant changes in attitude and behavior. This type of change frequently cuts through an organization's very essence. And since it requires the integration of many organizational subsystems, commitment must start at the level of senior management. They are the only group of people who have both the political clout and the position power to authorize modifications to such things as the reward system, the way jobs are designed, reporting relationships, and the like. Second, long-term change occurs only when there are sufficient numbers of champions and missionaries at *each* level of the organization. This concept of cascading commitment from champions (C) to missionaries (M) to impacted groups (I) is shown in Figure 7.5. It works best when you follow the formal chain of command. If you want to exert the maximum influence on a work group, you must have the strong commitment of that group's direct supervisor. Care should also be taken to avoid situations in which you select a champion to influence a group where no direct reporting relationship exists. This will usually result in significant conflict between the champion and the supervisor and/or members of the work group. This conflict over turf issues is a common outgrowth of organization politics.

Virtually every type of change project creates three distinct groups of people: the winners, the unaffected, and the losers. Those individuals who as a result of an initiative obtain enhanced status, responsibility, financial gains, or visibility are obviously the winners. For example, in an administrative productivity improvement initiative, the largest and most vocal groups of winners are the operating workforce. They usually

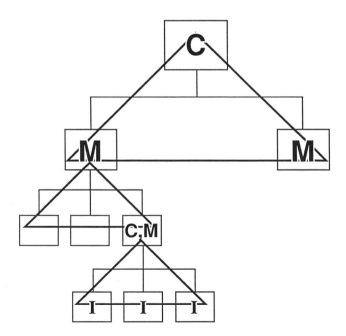

FIGURE 7.5. Cascading commitment in structural integration.

become more empowered in making decisions that affect them, and their jobs are redesigned to promote more challenge, variability, and the like.

If the scope of the productivity improvement initiative includes only "professional exempt" employees, the clerical support function will be either indirectly affected or untouched. Because of the minimal impact on the clerical workers, management should focus on communicating the "big picture" to them and making sure their expectations are realistic.

The individuals who are the biggest resisters of change are those who are the most negatively impacted. This is the group we label as the "losers." They are unfortunately the losers because they have lost prestige, money, political clout, or social status. It is important to realize that in most large-scale organizational change programs there are usually one or more groups of "losers." Therefore, special procedures or policies should be developed (outplacement assistance, re-education, job reassignment, etc.) to address this group equitably.

The biggest losers in an administrative productivity improvement program are typically the middle managers, the first-line supervisors, and those in administrative support functions. Middle managers lose because their kingdom is dispersed (their direct reports are assigned to other managers) and many of their positions are eliminated as spans of control are enlarged. The administrative support staff may also view themselves as losers because the operating workforce typically takes on a number of responsibilities (e.g., scheduling and quality inspections) that they previously performed. The biggest losers are usually first-line supervisors. These individuals typically perceive themselves as losing power, authority, and status. As more responsibilities are delegated to the operating workforce, it is not uncommon for supervisory spans of control to increase substantially, necessitating the displacement of first-line supervisors. The process of identifying and developing procedures to address the winners, losers, and unaffected groups equitably is called "environmental management."

"Individual integration" means selecting the most appropriate individuals to be internal change agents. Effective change agents must feel comfortable accepting risk. Risk taking is a function of structural and cultural factors and of individual characteristics. If an organization creates a culture that rewards calculated risk taking, provides adequate support systems such as education and participation, and provides sufficient resources, risk taking is encouraged. In addition to being comfortable with risk, effective change agents must have the appropriate skills and must be committed to undertaking the project.

There are times when senior management commitment to a project will be tested. The most likely scenario occurs when an old and tenured manager either will not or cannot (does not have the needed skills and personal attributes) to support an initiative. When this occurs, there are only two alternatives: to transfer or to terminate the individual. In most instances the options should follow the progressive sequence listed above. Unfortunately, there are times when a sense of urgency requires immediate termination. This is necessary because it communicates the strength of management's commitment to the initiative. It can also instill a certain amount of fear. Fear is analogous to stress. A stressless environment does not facilitate continuous improvement; rather, it tends to promote complacency. (If you doubt the validity of this statement, just compare the productivity of the Postal Service to that of Federal Express.) A certain amount of fear is good because it communicates a sense of urgency and increases the pain of nonaction.

Sometimes resistance is best eliminated by quick and decisive action. Another old Asian proverb comes to mind: "Select the largest nail that is sticking up and hammer it down." Sometimes all it takes to jumpstart a stalled initiative is to identify and fire one or more key managers or informal group leaders who are undermining the process. These "sacrificial lambs" send a clear and strong message about management's commitment to the program. This will motivate the remainder of the flock to fall into line.

Task 4: Identify Impacted Subsystems

The two preceding tasks focused on identifying those groups that would be impacted by the change program. In the present task the focus changes to determining how the change initiative will impact the organization's subsystems. Listed below are some of the subsystems commonly found in most organizations:

- Human resources.

- Planning and goal setting.
- Information.
- Organization design.
- Job design.
- Culture.

Figure 7.6 is an example of a completed worksheet for assessing the impact a Total Quality initiative has on an organization's subsystems. One would likely expect the culture, human resource systems, planning and goal setting system, and information system to be heavily impacted.

"Culture" is defined as the prevalent values, norms, assumptions, and beliefs within an organization. Depending on the size of the organization and the amount of differentiation, it is not uncommon to have an organizational culture and several subcultures. Subcultures can vary according to the organizational function (e.g., Manufacturing versus Finance) or by physical location (corporate, division, plant). Care must be exercised to assess the culture of any impacted population to determine the degree of fit between the planned initiative and the existing culture. It is important to identify any new attitudes, behaviors, or values the proposed change will require. This allows for the development of mechanisms (education, new reward systems, etc.) that will facilitate the transition. If significant differences exist between the culture and the proposed change, there are only two courses of action available:

1. Modify the culture to fit the initiative, or
2. Modify the initiative to better fit the culture.

It is not uncommon for organizations to approach change without ever ascertaining the fit between the culture and the initiative. We recently worked for an organization which had a culture that could be described as paternalistic, risk-averse, with a workforce that valued maintenance of the status quo. Employees had high needs for job security and preferred highly specialized jobs that were closely supervised. When the organization attempted to introduce an initiative that

Impacted Subsystems	Degree/Type of Impact	Potential Response
1. Human Resource Policies - Performance management - Reward system - Employee selection	Goals/objectives don't support a quality focus Current compensation system doesn't reward quality or customer satisfaction We look for individual performers not team players	Must modify division, unit, and individual goals Develop incentive system to reward quality focus Develop cross-functional teams
2. Performance measures	Current reporting system doesn't track correct quality attributes	Create new quality reporting system
3. Information system	Data integrity of current quality reporting system suspect	Identify software that will better meet business needs. Test / recommend purchase
4. Job design	Jobs highly specialized and repetitive	Utilize self-directed work teams
5. Organization design	Manufacturing organized into functional departments	Reorganize into focused factories with work teams
6. Other:		
Culture:	Current norms do not highly value customer satisfaction & quality	Develop education Displace managers who are not good role models

FIGURE 7.6. Completed worksheet for assessing impact on subsystems.

173

utilized work teams and required forced job rotation, World War III erupted. The culture and the change program were misaligned. The resulting program failed terribly: it was like putting a square peg into a round hole.

The human resource systems that would be heavily impacted by an initiative include the performance management system, the reward system, and employee selection procedures and criteria. Unit and individual performance measures would be altered to reflect a closer alignment to customer requirements. The reward system would probably reward employee flexibility. Employee selection critieria would focus on team process skills.

After the impacts on each subsystem are determined, a prioritized list of potential responses and options should be drawn up. This list will then be approved by management and become an input to a detailed design and implementation workplan.

Task 5: Identify Driving and Restraining Forces

During the last forty years a simple but powerful technique called "force field analysis" has been used to plan and manage organizational change. Force field analysis is based on the premise that two types of forces exist in every organization: driving and restraining forces. Driving forces are those people, policies, procedures, and other agents that support the change you are undertaking; restraining forces are those that run counter to the change. In order to develop enough momentum within an organization for change to occur, you have to maximize the driving forces and/or minimize the restraining forces. In most instances it is better to focus on minimizing the restraining forces. Attempts to maximize the driving forces are akin to pushing a cart rather than pulling it. The risk is that if you push too hard you can create new restraining forces.

In order to apply the powerful force field analysis technique to a change initiative, the following steps must be completed: (1) identify the problem and/or desired objective; (2) identify the driving and restraining forces; (3) prioritize the driving and restraining forces; (4) develop an action plan to eliminate or reduce those restraining forces that you have the authority to change.

Figure 7.7 illustrates how force field analysis can be used to identify

Problem/objective: *The current reward system does not support a World-Class Manufacturing program. A Skill-Based Pay reward system should be designed and implemented.*

Driving/restraining forces:

Priority	Driving forces
A_1	Senior management support
A_2	Poor organizational performance
B_1	Employees not happy with existing
	reward system
C	SBP successfully implemented
	in another SBU

Priority	Restraining forces
A_1	Existing collective bargaining
	agreement
B_1	No union support
B_2	Lack of employee understanding
B_3	No internal expertise on SBP

Figure 7.7.   Force field analysis.

the forces that support and constrain the development of a skill-based pay reward system that is designed to support a Total Quality initiative. Four driving and restraining forces are listed. In order of importance, the driving forces supporting the plan are senior management commitment, poor organizational performance during the last fiscal year, a workforce that is not satisfied with the existing reward system, and the successful implementation of a SBP program in another strategic business unit (SBU).

The key restraining forces in order of their importance are a restrictive collective bargaining agreement that does not lapse for another nine months, minimal support from the local union officials, poor employee understanding of skill-based pay, and the lack of internal subject matter experts to assist in the design and implementation of the program. Although the most important restraining force is the existing collective bargaining agreement, little can be done to circumvent this obstacle. But, since it will require almost eight months to design such a program, this restraining force is almost moot. One should therefore select restraining forces (minimal support from union officials, poor employee understanding of SBP) that *can* be impacted and develop an action plan to eliminate or minimize their adverse effects.

Potential action items to address the lack of union support and poor employee understanding of SBP are:

1. Schedule employee visits to several companies that have implemented successful skill-based pay reward systems.
2. Engage a consultant to work with union officials to improve their understanding of SBP concepts.
3. Develop education for the workforce that communicates the philosophy behind the program, plan components, and benefits to the employees and the organization.

Task 6: Develop an Implementation Plan

The first five tasks in our methodology focus on assessment. Each task has one or more products that become inputs into the development of a comprehensive change management workplan.

A large component of change management is project management. Initiatives such as JIT, administrative productivity improvement, and total quality management ripple throughout an organization. These initiatives impact a wide range of stakeholders and internal subsystems. Keeping track of the various action items can be a difficult and frustrating experience. We strongly recommend assigning a full-time project manager to ensure that details do not fall through the cracks. The success of any large-scale organization change project is directly related to the quality of project management.

The Japanese have a pungent way of describing the difference between Japanese and American management. They say American managers fire, adjust, fire, adjust, fire and adjust. They take pride in saying Japanese managers aim, aim, aim, and then fire. The key difference between approaches is that the Japanese tend to take more time during the planning process and *hit* what they are firing at! They believe Americans do not do enough assessment and that they make decisions without having thought out all of the contingencies.

Although it is beyond the scope of this book to teach project management principles, the following guidelines can facilitate the management of an initiative:

1. *Determine the appropriate scope of introduction (e.g., pilot, companywide) speed of introduction, and amount of employee involvement.* A set of variables that can be used to make this determination is given below.

- *Locus of expertise:* Who has the subject-matter expertise regarding the change initiative? Does it reside with senior management or within a particular function, or is it dispersed throughout the organization?

- *Existing culture:* What are the prevalent cultural characteristics? Specifically, does the culture promote stability or change?

- *Top management leadership style:* This refers not only to whether the prevalent leadership style is autocratic or participatory but also to management's skill in implementing change.

- *Clarity of the crisis:* This refers to the clarity and quality of communications regarding the business reason behind the change initiative. Is it perceived as a crisis or as an inconvenience?

- *Severity of crisis:* Does the crisis threaten the very future of the organization, or are the effects expected to be mild?

- *Likely resistance:* This relates to the anticipated level of resistance. If the crisis is clear and survival is threatened, significant resistance is less likely, and it may serve to your advantage as a rallying point for employees.

- *Size of organization:* If we compare the organization to a ship, it is easier to turn a destroyer than an aircraft carrier. A smaller organization is easier to keep focused and controlled during a transition.

This list of variables can be used to choose a set of strategies.

Suppose an organization has predominantly the following characteristics with respect to the seven variables: the senior management team has the needed expertise, the culture promotes risk-taking, the leadership style is autocratic, the need for change is highly visible, the crisis is severe, resistance is unlikely, and the organization is small. Then it should follow these strategies:

- Introduce the change using a wide scope.

- Introduce the change very quickly.

- Use employee involvement judiciously.

On the other hand, if the organization more closely fits the contrary profile—expertise dispersed, culture favoring stability, participatory leadership, need for change not clearly understood, crisis relatively mild, significant resistance likely, and organization large—then the antitheses of the above strategies should be followed. Specifically:

- Introduce the change using a narrow scope.

- Use a multiphased and deliberate approach.

- Utilize significant employee involvement in the design and implementation of the program.

The first strategy may seem to run counter to much of the current literature. Perhaps after we elaborate on the rationale, the logic of it will become clearer. Let us consider a hypothetical organization that is forced to implement an initiative because of threats to its survival from its external environment.

The XYZ company produces tricolored widgets. It is a fairly small (employs 125 people) and very traditionally managed (orders are given and people salute) organization that follows a "need to know" philosophy. During the last twelve months the company has experienced a considerable business downturn, leaving it in a precarious cash position. The comptroller has informed the president that the company has enough cash on hand to meet its obligations for the next three months. If it is not able to stop the bleeding within this period of time, it will be insolvent.

In an effort to take definitive actions, the senior management group engaged an outside consultant to identify the root causes of its performance shortfall. After a short assessment the consultant recommended the following actions that were agreed upon by the senior managment team: downsize and reduce the number of management layers, reduce inventory, and begin the transition to JIT.

Since the downsizing would generate the most cash in the short term, management decided to focus their initial efforts on supporting this initiative. Since management had the vast majority of the expertise relevant to the cost drivers within the organization, they planned and implemented the transition using a top–down power-holding strategy. Since the crisis was apparent to all employees and obviously survival-threatening, time did not afford significant opportunities for involvement. If management took the time to create committees, conduct education, and so on, the doors would probably close before the initiative was implemented. Since the organization was small and manageable and the employees were accustomed to being told what to do, resistance was likely to be mild to moderate.

Does this hypothetical organization sound familiar? Although it is certainly not the norm, there are occasions when change must occur swiftly, using a centralized rather than decentralized decision-making approach. In these special situations, change must be mandated to ensure that at least some forces survive to fight another day.

2. *Organize the project.* It is important, early on, to clarify the structure of the project team. Depending on the type of initiative and its scope of impact, it is common to have a multi-tiered project organization (usually a management advisory group and one or more employee teams). The upper tier should be comprised of senior managers from each functional unit that is impacted. Their role is to obtain cross-functional cooperation, provide direction to the program, and approve deliverables. A project management team is also frequently used to attend to the day-to-day details of design and implementation. These teams are usually composed of a vertical cross-section of employees from all affected groups. They are responsible for carrying out each action item in the workplan. Tasks can range from data collection and analysis to education of the workforce.

3. *Develop the detailed workplan* (see Figure 7.8). This includes brainstorming a list of all tasks and, if appropriate, subdividing them

Phase/Segment/Task/Step	Resp	Resources	Deliver-ables	Start Date	Comp. Date
PHASE I: ORGANIZATION ASSESSMENT					
SEGMENT: PROJECT ORGANIZATION					
Task 1.0 Est. Management Advisory Group (MAG)					
Step 1.1 Identify Roles/Responsibilities					
• Define objective and scope					
• Secure cross functional cooperation					
• Review & approve deliverables					
• Review & approve implementation plan					
• Est. priorities for steps in imp. plan					
Step 1.2 Select Group Members (include rep. from every function impacted). Overlap with change mgt. team					
• Senior mgt., union leaders, involve union ASAP					
Step 1.3 Select Chairperson					
Task 2.0 Est. Change Management Team					
Step 2.1 Identify Roles/Responsibilities					
• Day to day project mgt.					
• Collect and analyze data					
• Identify, design, and implement needed interventions					
• Communicate project to workforce					
• Solicit imput from workforce					
Step 2.2 Select Group Members (vertical cross of all employees impacted)					
• HR Rep., change agents, middle management, internal consultants, trainers, first line supv., employees					
Step 2.3 Select Project Manager					
Task 3.0 Finalize Change Approach					
Step 3.1 Finalize Workplan for Phase I					
• Scope, objective, approach,					
• Products, deliverables					
Step 3.2 Establish Admin. Control Procedures					
Task 4.0 Develop Communication Strategy					
Step 4.1 Identify Communication Channels					
• Banners, payroll stuffers, committees, videotapes, meetings, publications, task forces, bulletin boards, Q&A sessions, etc.					
• Focus on setting realistic expectations					

Figure 7.8. Example of a detailed workplan.

into steps. The tasks should then be sequenced into their chronological order. Resources (facilities, personnel, equipment, and materials) should then be identified for each task and step. This will facilitate budget development. Once this is done, the deliverables/products should be identified along with assigned responsibilities and starting and completion dates for each task and step.

4. *Monitor and revise the plan.* This final step includes analyzing the project's status on an ongoing basis, identifying potential problems, and modifying the plan accordingly.

Task 7: Implement Change and Evaluate

If sufficient time and effort were expended during the planning process, implementation will occur smoothly. Before one actually begins implementation, it is important to confirm the organization's level of readiness to accept the change. The following are several questions that can be used to confirm organizational readiness:

1. Has the vision been clearly communicated to all stakeholders?
2. Have rewards, recognition, and/or punishments been established to maximize compliance?
3. Have interventions been chosen and designed to ensure that the organization's subsystems closely support the change initiative?
4. Where appropriate, are affected stakeholders actively involved in the design and implementation of the initiative?
5. Has a critical mass of commitment been created throughout the organization?
6. Has timely and targeted education been provided?
7. Are there sufficient resources to implement the initiative without adversely affecting ongoing operations?

If these issues have been addressed, implementation merely consists of developing one or more vertical, cross-functional implementation teams. Each team should have a clearly defined structure, with a team leader. In addition, the teams should have defined roles, responsibilities, and limits of decision-making authority. Once this has been done, conflict management or problem-resolution procedures can be developed to address unplanned contingencies.

Evaluation is an ongoing component of implementation. It typically includes obtaining several measurements along a predetermined schedule and comparing baselines to interim/terminal objectives. Opportunities for improvement are then identified and incorporated into the design plan. Conceptually, the evaluation process should focus on identifying problems in *sufficient time* to take *corrective action*.

In order for program evaluation to be effective, a host of administrative control procedures must be developed. These procedures will address such things as the type of data collection methods used, the frequency of evaluation, the types of evaluation criteria that will be used (QWL, operational, attitudinal), variance analysis procedures, and management reporting requirements.

Task 8: Institutionalize the Change

The average employee today is more informed and more perceptive than ever before. Management must "walk the talk" in all of its actions and directives because employees have become adept at recognizing the disparity between what is said and what is done. The greater the disparity, the greater the distrust. If employees believe management has a hidden agenda or is not committed, they will perceive the initiative as another one of those programs that will go away after a short time.

Institutionalizing the change is akin to burning the bridges so people can't go back to doing things the "old" way. It is here that the people management systems must be modified to closely support the change initiative. It is essential that the planning and goal setting process, performance measures, control systems, and human resource systems closely support the change plan.

Chapter **8**

Summary

We hope that this book has broadened your awareness. The problems and obstacles faced by most manufacturing companies in the United States are numerous. Our global competition is formidable. Our future standard of living is potentially at risk of compromise. No one trick is going to save the day for any manufacturing company. We hope that we have been successful in sensitizing you to the actions necessary to remain competitive in today's environment. There is unquestionably a need for an approach that balances the company's business, technology, and people systems.

We have compiled the best practices demonstrated by some of the manufacturing world's front-runners. The theories and principles that are common to many of their operations are not mysterious. High quality, efficient productivity, and super use of people are probably as basic a business philosophy as you can get. But the simple fact is that many companies have lost sight of these fundamentals. Businesses have grown in size and complexity to the point where they seem almost unmanageable. The companies that kid themselves into thinking that complex rules and hierarchies will govern their direction will be strangled by the loss of reactive flexibility and the weight of their own bureaucracy. Communication is, in our experience, deficient in many organizations. The greater the number of people, the more difficult communication becomes. Bigger is not better.

An executive we have worked with once said, "Common sense is anything but." The truth of these words rings crystal clear. Rarely do we address a management group that does not understand the impact of the changes happening in the manufacturing sector. But amazingly few recognize the disparity between what they are doing and what they should be doing. Most are too close to the problem to see what's wrong. Those that do recognize deficiencies often are unable to be objective about what needs to be done. It is human to be afraid of the unknown. Very few of us like change, and yet we all understand its necessity.

We would like to share some valuable advice of Joseph E. Izzo that is quoted in the May 1991 issue of *Manufacturing Systems:*

> If you must make a journey through an uncharted wilderness, take a worthy guide who has made the trip before. When your journey is completed you will have learned respect for the wilderness, wisdom from your guide, and resourcefulness from within yourself. Make the journey alone or with an unworthy guide and you will learn only the fear of being lost.

Many of the points we have made in this book are more than theory. They have been proven by the pioneers who set out to change the rules of the manufacturing game. The knowledge, experience, and benefits these companies have gained demonstrate the power of effective application of the new methods. They have succeeded to the point where competitors must change the way they operate. Why? Because the judges are the world's consumers and they are demanding the satisfaction and performance levels the new generation of suppliers are providing.

Time is the only thing every competitor, in every market, possesses equally. How that time is used determines how successful any company will be. It is a waste of time to cry about competitors who are not playing fair. There can be no "fair," because the winners keep changing the way the game is played. A company trying to compete by using yesterday's rules, regardless of its reputation or skill, will not survive long. The first company to strike a market from a new angle will be in a position to redefine how everyone else will play. The leaders will burst through the envelope that defines the limits of performance and value. Lethargic companies will continue to be victimized by more agile competitors leveraging time.

Our mission has been to help companies focus on organizing and harnessing the capability of the workforce to drive their operations. The workers, at every level of the organization, will determine the quality of the products and how efficiently time is used. The best management desire and intent will be futile if the company cannot organize and motivate its people to push beyond the limit. The flaw in past initiatives has always been the same: lack of commitment and/or lack of discipline. Real commitment and "ownership" of the initiative must be inherent at every level of the company. The unfortunate reality is that not everyone cares equally about the company. Don't blame the least interested folks until you fully understand their environment and motivation.

Perhaps the best gauge of how serious a company is about change is its willingness to correct inequities. Do not discount the organizational impact that the perverse compensation differential between the top (the haves) and the bottom (the have nots) has on the "teams" many companies have attempted to develop. If management is willing to recognize the facts and implement changes, which may translate into personal sacrifices, then true excellence is both achievable and sustainable. If management is not willing to make the really tough changes, then any improvements will be limited by the bounds of the selflessness and patience of the employees. It is equity, and not necessarily equality, that is the mandatory foundation of success for any team.

We wish you the best of luck in your pursuit of world-class excellence. Remember that what seems obvious will not be easy. Your ability to advance depends on two factors:

- Balance in the approach.
- Discipline in execution.

Without these two elements, the campaign will flounder and produce limited results. The staying power of the changes depends on how well the new initiatives have been institutionalized throughout the organization by the critical mass of employees. Do not violate the entropy principle. Survival necessitates the constant input of energy in the form of attention, time, and money.

Time must be the new management touchstone. It will either be your company's strongest ally or its worst enemy. Focus your energy and resources on reducing the time it takes do anything within your company. If you are effective in eliminating waste, the results will be higher-quality products, processes, and people; improved productivity and higher profit will come as natural consequences of these. Finally, keep in mind that it is not necessary to learn all of life's lessons on your own. There is no shame in seeking advice or assistance from outside your organization. There is shame only in defeat.

Bibliography

Belcher, John. "Gainsharing: Designed for Success." *The Productivity Brief* (May 1986).

Block, Peter. "Empowering Employees." *Training and Development Journal* (April 1987): 30-40.

Bullock, R., and Edward Lawler III. "Incentives and Gainsharing Stimuli for Productivity." American Productivity Center, 1986.

Christopher, Robert. *The Japanese Mind.* New York: Fawcett Columbine, 1983.

Collins, Samuel. "Incentive Programs: Pros and Cons." *Personnel Journal* (July 1981): 571-75.

Connor, Darryl. *Building Synergistic Work Teams.* Atlanta: OD Resources, 1985.

Doty, D. "Pay for Knowledge Compensation Systems and Macro Organizational Variables." The University of Texas at Austin.

Eklund, Christopher. "How A & P Fattens Profits by Sharing Them." *Business Week* (December 1987).

Fein, Mitchell. "Let's Return to MDW for Incentives." *Industrial Engineer* (January 1979): 34-37.

——— *Wage Incentive Plans.* Norcross, GA: American Institute of Industrial Engineers, 1980.

———— *Improshare: An Alternative to Traditional Managing.* Norcross, GA: American Institute of Industrial Engineers, 1981.

———— "Improved Productivity through Worker Involvement." *Industrial Management* (1982): 4-15.

Gabrib, Gerald, Kenneth Mitchell, and Ronald Mclemore. "Rewarding Individual and Team Productivity: The Biloxi Merit Bonus Plan." *Public Personnel Management* (Fall 1985).

Goggin, Zane. "Two Sides of Gainsharing." *Management Accounting* (October 1986): 47-50.

Halcomb, Ruth. "Aerospace Awards." *Incentive Marketing* (December 1985).

Hardy, John, Bruce Orton, and Weldon Moffit. "Bonus Systems Do Motivate." *Management Accounting* (November 1986): 58-61.

Heyel, Carl, ed. *The Encyclopedia of Management.* 3rd ed. New York: Van Nostrand and Reinhold, 1982.

Hills, F., et al. "Merit Pay Just or Unjust Desserts." *Personnel* (1983).

"Job Enrichment in General Foods." *European Industrial Relations Review* (November 1974).

Johansen, Per, and Kenneth McGuire. *Continuous Improvement.* Cambridge, MA: Rudra Press, 1986.

Kelly, Don, and Daryl Conner. "The Emotional Cycle of Change" in *1979 Annual Handbook for Group Facilitation.* San Diego: University Associates.

Lawler, Edward, III. "The Design of Effective Award Systems." USC Graduate School of Business Administration, 1982.

———— "Pay for Performance: A Motivational Analysis." USC Graduate School of Business Administration, 1983.

———— "What Ever Happened to Incentive Pay?" USC Graduate School of Business Administration, 1983.

———— "Paying for Organizational Performance." USC Graduate School of Business Administration, 1988.

Lehman, David. "Improving Employee Productivity Through Incentives." *Journal of Systems Management* (March 1986): 14-20.

Lentz, G. "Implementing Pay for Knowledge in Existing and Unionized Organizations." Paper presented at the Academy of Management Meeting, San Diego, 1985.

MacDonnell, Arthur. "This Incentive Plan Teaches Employees How to Participate." *New England Business Journal* (March 1983).

McGuire, Kenneth. *Impressions from Our Most Worthy Competitor.* Falls Church, VA: American Production and Inventory Control Society, 1984.

McLean, J. "How CEO Led in Sales Evolution that Doubled Deposits." *Bank Marketing* (October 1985).

Metzger, Bert. *Elements of a Sharing Participative System.* Chicago: Profit Sharing Research Foundation, 1977.

———— "Profit Sharing as a System Incentive." Speech presented at Work in America Conference on Sharing Gains of Productivity, Evanston, 1977.

———— *Improving Productivity and the QWL Through Financial Participation Programs.* Chicago: Profit Sharing Research Foundation, 1981.

Moffat, Susan. "Picking Japan's Research Brains." *Fortune* (March 25, 1991): 84-96.

Mohrman, S. "Employee Participation Programs: Implications for Productivity Improvement." *The Industrial Organizational Psychologist* (1986): 38-43.

Myor, Michael. "An Employee Incentive Program That Has Some Real Bite." *Bank Marketing* (December 1985).

O'Dell, Carla. "So You Want to Install a Gainsharing System: Answers to 12 Commonly Asked Questions." *The Productivity Brief* 1 (6): 1-4.

———— *Gainsharing Involvement, Incentives, and Productivity.* New York: AMACOM, 1981.

O'Dell, Carla, and Jerry McAdams. "The Revolution in Employee Rewards." *Management Review* (March 1987).

Peters, Tom. *Thriving on Chaos.* New York: Alfred A. Knopf, 1987.

Recardo, Ronald. "JIT With Two R's: Reward and Recognition." *Target Journal* (Summer 1989).

———— "Administrative Productivity Improvement: The Next Frontier." *The Journal for Quality and Participation* 12 (1990).

———— "Appropriate Reward Systems for a JIT Environment." *Journal for Quality and Participation* 12 (1990).

———— "Change Management: The What, the Why, and the How." *Manufacturing Systems* (May 1991).

Reuter, Vincent. "Wage Incentives: A Valued Management Tool." *Industrial Management* (July-August 1985): 25-29.

Ross, Timothy, and Ruth Ross. "The Multiple Benefits of Gainsharing." *Personnel Journal* (October 1986): 14-25.

Savage, John. "Incentive Programs at Nucor Corporation Boost Productivity." *Personnel Administration* (August 1981): 33-40.

Schuster, Michael. "Gainsharing Opportunities and Threats." *The Boardroom Reports* (October 1987).

——— "Gainsharing: Do It Right the First Time." *Sloan Management Review* (Winter 1987): 17-25.

Solomon, Barbara Anne. "When Incentives Add Punch to Production Line Pay." *Personnel* (September 1983).

Stalk, George. "Time—The Next Source of Competitive Advantage." *Harvard Business Review* (July-August 1988): 41-51.

Tosi, H., and L. Tosi. "Knowledge Based Pay: Some Propositions and Guides to Effective Use." Cornell University.

U.S. Department of Labor. *Exploratory Investigation of Pay for Knowledge Systems.* Washington, DC: U.S. Department of Labor, 1986.

Walton, Richard. "The Topeka Work System: Optimistic Visions, Pessimistic Hypothesis and Reality." *The Wharton Magazine* (Spring 1978).

WoJahn, Ellen. "Gainfully Employed." *Inc.* (December 1983): 150-54.

Index